The Work of Faith

Real faith
taken to a whole new level

True stories by:
Robin M. Hailey

A GOSHEN PUBLISHERS BOOK   VIRGINIA

The Work of Faith
Real faith taken to a whole new level

ISBN: 978-0-9994003-4-0
Copyright ©2019 Robin M. Hailey

Library of Congress Cataloging-in-Publication Data

Published in 2019 by:

GOSHEN PUBLISHERS LLC
P.O. Box 1562
Stephens City, Virginia, USA
www.GoshenPublishers.com

Our books may be purchased in bulk for promotional, educational, or business use. For inquiries please contact the publisher via email: Agents@GoshenPublishers.com.

First Edition 2019

Cover designed by Goshen Publishers LLC

Printed in the United States of America

All Scriptures are quoted from the King James Version of the Bible unless otherwise noted.

Dedication

This book is dedicated to:
The God of Abraham, Isaac, and Jacob
who, according to Romans 12:3,
"hath dealt to every man
the measure of faith."

Preface

The day that I changed my thinking, awe-inspiring things began to happen. Under many circumstances, I had to keep silent during the process and only divulge what God had done after His perfect will had been performed. Sometimes, if you share details with people, they kill your dream, distract your focus, or steal your vision.

One thing is certain; if God gave the plan to you, an imitation will not succeed. If your dream in the eyes of man appears to be absurd, they will try to talk you out of it or cloud your mind with, "If I were you," comments. Any time you allow doubt to come in, regardless of how high the adversary turns up the heat, you are setting yourself up for disappointment because you are failing to allow God to be in charge.

I began writing this book in 1996, and as different events occurred, some pleasant and others unpleasant, I put the book aside, but the necessity to complete it kept ringing out in my spirit. During a prophetic impartation service with our pastor, Apostle Vernon Huffman, the Lord spoke through him specifically to me; God said, "Write the book!" All I could do was smile for I knew those words came straight from the third Heaven (Deu 10:14; 1 Kin 8:27). Apostle Huffman had only been our pastor for less than two years and I had never mentioned at any time that I had notes associated with an unfinished book.

Over subsequent weeks, I developed an urgency to get moving and complete this task. The initial challenge began when I could not find the original disk. Believe it or not, it was a three-and-a-half-inch floppy. Now, how obsolete is that? With that being said, I had to take my fragmented, hand-written notes and start from the beginning.

My prayer is that each reader becomes enlightened with the realization that God is the same yesterday, today, and forever. He is a God who is no respecter of persons. Your faith in Him can make the impossible possible and defy the laws of nature. Everyone will not be willing to understand nor agree with your faith walk, especially when the immediate circumstances appear to be hopeless. Be encouraged to hold on to your faith, even if it means the journey is only between you and God.

As you read this book, understand that it has been written from a very personal standpoint. I am not accustomed to being this transparent but if it helps others, to God be the Glory.

You will smile with me, cry with me, and sometimes shout, "Hallelujah!" with me. There were times I had to stop writing because I could not go on any further. Looking at things displayed in such detail became overwhelming for me as the writer, but I know this book will change many lives for years to come.

Shalom,
R. M. Hailey

Table of Contents

1. Faith, the Substance

Faith is a firm belief in something where there is no tangible or visible substantiation. Unwavering faith is steadfast even when situations seem to be going contrary to the promises of God. Hebrews 11:1 says, "Now faith is the substance of things hoped for, the evidence of things not seen." People must personally believe in what cannot be seen with their natural eyes and allow their exhibition of faith to bring about what may appear to be impossible.

I think about the woman who had an issue of blood for 12 years (Matt 9:20-22). She had faith to

> (1) defy tradition by going into the midst of the crowd knowing that she was considered unclean; and then

> (2) reach out and touch the hem of Jesus' garment. "For she said within herself, If I may but touch his garment, I shall be whole" (v21).

She did not stop at just having a thought, but she put it into action. Despite all the people in the crowd, her touch was different from anyone else's because Jesus perceived virtue had gone out (Luke 8:46). "But Jesus turned him about, and when he saw her, he said, Daughter, be of good comfort; thy faith hath made thee whole. And the woman was made whole from that hour" (Matt 9:22). It was not the touch that made her whole; it was her faith.

Faith maintains its own attributes and cannot be compared with anything else; whereas a belief can be proven either true or false. Faith cannot be measured through mathematics or by scientific testing. Faith causes things to occur that just don't make sense in the natural. Occurrences such as the unexplainable make people stand back and scratch their heads, because in order to understand a phenomenon one must step out of the natural into the supernatural.

People who do not understand the significance of faith, will see a faith walker as someone in denial and, possibly, someone not in touch with reality. A faith walker is someone who will not focus on his or her current situation or circumstance but will prepare for the blessing that is not yet visible with the natural eye.

When you are amidst a trying situation with no tangible options, activate your faith and watch it work for you. Sometimes when you find yourself in a scary position you must trust God on a level you've never had to, especially when time is of the essence and you have no contingency plan.

Remember 2 Timothy 1:7, "For God hath not given us the spirit of fear; but of power, and of love, and of a sound mind." Bind the feeling of fear in the blessed name of Jesus and release strength to encourage yourself to not be discouraged by what you may see.

In 1 Samuel (30:1-6), David and his men returned to Ziglag, found it destroyed by fire and the Amalekites had taken the women and children captive, the men wanted to stone him. Rather than getting absorbed by the discourse his men were spreading, he took a different route and encouraged himself in the Lord God. Once you have experienced the work of faith, you'll be persuaded to employ faith on a higher level.

Each level comes with its own process, but previous victories provide the steppingstones.

Speaking as one who truly relies on God, I have learned that when you have done all you can to be obedient to Him; yet, your world appears to be falling apart all around you, all you can do is stand. You cannot focus on what appears to be real; instead, trust God through the test and the reward in the end will be greater than you could have fathomed.

Faith consists of three parts: knowledge, assent, and then trust.

> *Knowledge* comes through your previous experience with faith and understanding that what you believed for will come to pass.
>
> *Assent* is where you are officially in agreement with or approve an idea, plan, or request. Regarding biblical faith, you base your actions upon what you agree with as represented in God's Word.
>
> *Trust* is the last component of faith and is a firm belief that, come hell or high water, God will bring you out with total victory because your confidence in Him is unwavering.

Faith must be exercised daily in order for it to accomplish what you desire; you cannot take faith on a roller coaster ride and achieve desired results. Continuity must be present in your walk of faith. A life without faith is almost like a life without food. Hebrews 11:1 states that faith becomes the evidence of what we cannot see. If you can see it and you can determine the outcome, then it's not faith.

The belief in faith becomes a paradox or mockery to those who think they have the ability to make things happen on their own, or they can develop an alternate plan without waiting upon God to divinely intervene. We are not to lean to our own understanding (Prov 3:5). Allow God to do something

He has never done before. Allow God to get the glory. And, don't become anxious or impatient. Remember that it will be in His timing, not ours.

For example, in Exodus (17:1-4) the people of Israel complained to Moses because there was no water and accused him of bringing them out of Egypt to die in the wilderness. First, God's people had never been outside the walls of Egypt and had soon forgotten the miracle that took place freeing them from slavery. Second, although they came out of Egypt, as time passed, we see in the Scriptures that Egypt had not come out of them. Moses cried to the Lord because of the headache the people were creating, and the Lord answered. Moses was instructed to go to the rock at Horeb and strike it (Exo 17:6). By faith, Moses did as God commanded in the presence of the elders and the rock released water. God wanted the people to see that they were not forsaken, and they needed to stop quarrelling with Moses who was carrying faith for all the children of Israel, which totaled an astronomical number of people.

In Numbers (20:2-5), Moses and his brother Aaron ran into a similar situation in the desert of Zin. The entire congregation of people came against both Moses and Aaron because there was no water. "And Moses and Aaron went from the presence of the assembly unto the door of the tabernacle of the congregation, and they fell upon their faces: and the glory of the LORD appeared unto them. And the LORD spake unto Moses, saying, Take the rod, and gather thou the assembly together, thou, and Aaron thy brother, and speak ye unto the rock before their eyes; and it shall give forth his water, and thou shalt bring forth to them water out of the rock: so thou shalt give the congregation and their beasts drink" (v6-8).

Unfortunately, Moses let his anger against the disobedient bunch of people get the best of him and he disobeyed God and struck the rock, not once but twice (v11).

Nevertheless, God still provided water for everyone, but this action came at a great cost to Moses (v12).

There are times when you can say, "Oops!" and fix the transgression but that was not the case for Moses. His lack of self-control and disobedience caused his faith to become fractured leading to insubordination against God and ultimately denying him the right to step foot into the promised land (Deu 34:1-4).

My point with these examples is to reiterate the importance of maintaining your faith and trust in God. Not only is faith a requirement, but also, we are to pursue with perseverance our desire to have more of God and then maintain a rock-solid relationship with Him. Seal your faith with works. Show God that you do not plan to fold under pressure but will continue to stand. God is aware of our challenges, our limitations, and our possible breaking points, but we hold an obligation to exercise the faith that we so freely speak about.

Our daily walk should be geared by faith (2 Cor 5:7) and with a willingness to please God. According to Hebrews 11:6, "But without faith it is impossible to please him: for he that cometh to God must believe that he is, and that he is a rewarder of them that diligently seek him." We must be willing to lay aside every weight that has the potential to interfere with our walk in Christ (Col 2:6). Sometimes that weight can be other people, past hurt, past disappointments, and our own past failures.

For greater results, there are times you may have to fortify your faith with the Word of God. This will allow you to push past obstacles that the adversary placed in your way to discourage you from moving forward. Faith without works is dead (Jam 2:26) and, in some cases, your work is to verbalize the Word of God by speaking the Word into the atmosphere. Take the logos word, the written word, and make it a Rhema by speaking it.

One day I was led to create a page of Bible verses specifically to use as affirmation statements. I must say they had a more profound effect on how my day went then I could have envisioned. In the correct order, the Scriptures supported each other and, in turn, encouraged and strengthened me. The Word was my personal character-building tool. Hebrews (5:12) states, "For the word of God is quick, and powerful, and sharper than any two-edged sword, piercing even to the dividing asunder of soul and spirit, and of the joints and marrow, and is a discerner of the thoughts and intents of the heart." Let the Word become your spiritual sword.

Here, I would like to share a testimony of a Word of faith in action. Lack of health insurance caused me to skip mammogram examinations for many years. I was finally able to schedule and have one performed. A few days afterwards, I received a letter from Radiology that I needed to return for further testing but nothing specific was indicated. At first my heart dropped, but then I declared, "The devil is a liar, nothing alarming will be found." I began believing God right then and there that no abnormality existed. I immediately called the radiologist and scheduled an appointment. I refused to allow fear to cause me to procrastinate.

In the meantime, my primary care physician called, and she was very upset. I guessed she was having nightmares as she remembered the trauma, I went through with my left leg in 2011. Not wanting to experience another serious situation with the same patient, she was frantic. She was there when I was admitted with a swollen leg that no longer looked like it belonged to a human. I proclaimed then that I serve the God of Abraham, the God of Isaac, and the God of Jacob (Matt 22:32). He is the God of the living. She was amazed in subsequent months as I regained my independence and was able to drive to my own appointments. The doctor, who happens to be of the Jewish religion, had never experienced that kind of move of God; nor had she experienced such an exhibition of faith in Yahweh, who is a miracle working God.

I told my doctor that a follow-up appointment had been made with Radiology and I knew all was well. Now, I go back to the topic of denial. To profess all to be well regarding the mammogram and return for additional testing, were acts of faith; but, to allow fear to overtake me and to not go back would be denial. Faith in action is to believe what has not yet been confirmed. Denial is to ignore what you have been made aware of and then decline the opportunity to dispel what the adversary is trying to inflict upon you.

At the appointed time, I went back to the radiologist, Linda, who took images of my right side only. After a close examination of the new images and comparing them with the previous set, she said, "I need to discuss something with the doctor."

I could see concern on her face, but I did not let it bother me. What I later came to realize was that she had the look of bewilderment. When she left the room, it gave me a private moment to have a personal talk with God. I prayed, "God, out of all that my body has gone through even before the leg incident, I don't believe any type of breast issue is part of my destiny. You said I still have a lot of work to do in support of kingdom building and I know it doesn't involve me running back and forth to the hospital for any kind of treatment. So, I humble myself before you Lord and place my impending situation in your hands."

Linda returned and said, "Honey, I really hate to do this, but I need to take a few more images and apply more pressure than normal."

I told her, "I don't mind, do what you need to do, but know this one thing, all is well."

Sure enough, after she took the second set of images and whatever she saw the first time was no longer there. Her comment was, "It must have burst because it is gone."

I guess that was the only way she could articulate what had just happened. I'm quite sure she did see something that threw up a flag as it did during the previous appointment but the outcome as a witness to the power of faith in God was, there is nothing negative to report.

I told her, "Like I said, all is well."

If I didn't have faith to believe it is well, and strengthen my faith by speaking into the atmosphere, that, "It is well", the attempt of the adversary to attack my body would not have been rendered null and void.

Hearing my belief in the power of prayer led her to ask me to pray for her daughter. She wasn't specific in what was going on with her little girl, but I could tell from the tone in her voice, she had a sincere concern. I assured her, as led by the Spirit of God, that I would pray for her. My primary doctor is in the same building as Radiology. Every time I have an appointment, I stop by the first floor but it's never on a day Linda is in the building. I leave a message with the receptionist that the intercessor is still praying for her daughter.

We should understand that sometimes we don't go through situations for ourselves, but it's to be a blessing to another. Don't let your circumstance distract you from seeing the bigger picture. Remember that God has a purpose for everything. He will use your situation to allow you to cross the path of someone who needs an encouraging word to make it through what they are trying to endure. This is where Romans (8:28) comes in for it says, "And we know that all things work together for good to them that love God, to them who are the called according to his purpose." Once we come to understand God's purpose, it puts things into a better perspective, and we can see things the way He does.

2. Faith through the Word

The Word of God is an authoritative tool providing spiritual ammunition that can be used to fight against mind attacks that have been sent from the camp of the adversary. The Word is also a source of encouragement when circumstances appear to be overwhelming and there is no one around to uplift you.

Many of our actions, whether positive or negative, begin with a thought. Permitting the Word of God to retain an active part of our everyday lives keeps us on track with God. Psalm 119:105 depicts the word as, "a lamp unto my feet, and a light unto my path." Allowing God's word to light your path will keep you from mentally, and potentially physically, walking into dark places.

David wrote, "Thy word have I hid in mine heart, that I might not sin against thee" (Psa 119:11). He didn't proclaim that he would never sin, but declared that he was less likely to sin because God's word was hidden in his heart. Faith has a greater opportunity to take root in your inner man when you hide God's Word in the deep chambers of your heart. The more familiar you become with the Word, the greater the understanding you acquire of who God is to you. It is difficult to maintain a relationship with someone with whom you don't spend any time. For example, if you don't spend quality time with your spouse or significant other, he or she will go elsewhere. God is a gentleman and will never force Himself on an individual, but will patiently wait for the individual to seek Him out.

Just to show how powerful the Word is, John (1:1) tells us, "In the beginning was the Word, and the Word was with God, and the Word was God." This signifies the Word was in the beginning before the first chapter of Genesis. John (1:14) tells us, "And the Word was made flesh, and dwelt among us (and we beheld his glory, the glory as of the only begotten of the Father), full of grace and truth."

The Word can be nothing less than powerful because Paul picked up a mystery in 1 Timothy (3:16) when he stated, "And without controversy great is the mystery of godliness: God was manifest in the flesh, justified in the Spirit, seen of angels, preached unto the Gentiles, believed on in the world, received up into glory."

If the Word, through the manifestation of God, had the power to become flesh, just think what can occur when we take that same Word by faith, whose power has already been demonstrated and use it to overpower the works of Satan. The same Word will allow us to, "call those things which be not as though they were" (Rom 4:17). By giving us His Word, God has given us the same authority. Even Jesus encouraged his disciples when they marveled at what they saw Him do. In John (14:12), He told them for those who believed in Him, greater works shall they do because He's going to the Father.

When quoting Scriptures, I primarily use the King James Version because it is my preferred version and the one with which I am most familiar, but at times I may refer to a different version to obtain a fuller understanding. Hebrews 4:12 (KJV) says, "For the word of God is quick, and powerful, and sharper than any two-edged sword." The Living Bible says, "For whatever God says to us is full of power." Anything living by the power of Almighty God's Word can withstand anything and through faith in God, so can we.

Staying in the Word of God will make you more sensitive to your surroundings. When you sense things are not right, you will know if you're required to leave that location, get involved, or if God needs you there to pray and change the atmosphere. Understand your purpose for being there and allow God to give you instructions.

During His 40-day fast in the desert, Jesus simplistically used the Word of His Heavenly Father while being tempted by the devil (Matt 4:1-11) and did the same in various other passages of Scripture when confronted by the Scribes and Pharisees. Matthew 23 contains what is known as the eight woes (vs 13, 14, 15, 16, 23, 25, 27 and 29). You don't always have to use long, complicated, and impressive words, just God's Word backed by faith.

God's Word gives us power to bind the devil, cancel his assignment, and send him to the dry place. Then, in return, loose blessings upon the areas that have been previously under attack. When you bind something, loose something positive to replace it, otherwise you leave that spot empty and unguarded. Matthew (16:19b), "and whatsoever thou shalt bind on earth shall be bound in heaven: and whatsoever thou shalt loose on earth shall be loosed in heaven." Once again, we have the power.

Satan's plan is to keep so much turmoil going on around us that we forget to use the Word of God. His ploy is nothing but an attempt to disrupt God's flow. We must consistently utilize the Word in order to maintain a successful faith walk. Continuity is the key. Don't become distracted.

> Always purpose in your heart to give God your best and never give Him leftovers.

3. Tithing Fundamentals

Your faith has the ability to move mountains. Sometimes you need to evaluate in which category your faith belongs. Do you have great faith like the Centurion in Matthew (8:10), little faith as Matthew (8:26) captured the event when Jesus rebuked the sea, or no faith as Mark (4:40) also wrote about the disciple's fear and Jesus rebuking the sea? I ask this because there is a course of action to giving tithes.

The first biblical documentation of tithing can be found in Genesis (14:20-21) where Abram blessed Melchizedek after returning from the slaughter of their enemies. He presented the high priest with a tenth part of his increase. The giving of tithes was mentioned again in Hebrews (7:1-2) where the writer states, "To whom also Abraham gave a tenth part of all; first being by interpretation King of righteousness, and after that also King of Salem, which is, King of peace."

In the Old Testament, God's people were required to give 10% of everything they earned. Their giving came from the land and their herds or flock (Lev 27:30-32). Paul wrote, "On the first day of every week each one of you is to put something aside, in proportion to his prosperity, and save it so that no collections [will need to] be made when I come," (1 Cor 16:2, retrieved from the Amplified Version on BibleGateway.com).

Our society is money based. Tithes should, therefore, come off your gross income and not your net. Your giving should be in accordance with your income and correspond in nature with Abram's tithe to Melchizedek.

The gross is your income before taxes; the net is what you have left after deductions. Some people hear this and the financial games begin.

If your gross for a pay period is $2,500, 10% = $250; if your gross pay for a pay period is $750 then your tithe would be $75, etc. Understandably, the government takes their money off the top. They do this because some people cannot be trusted to pay when it is due. When you tithe, don't forget to ask God to sanctify and multiply your remaining 90% balance. Surprisingly, this action will extend that which remains.

Don't fall into the trap of playing with the numbers and submit the amount from your net as your tithe. That is the same as telling God that the government is more important than He is, and you doubt His Word. Tithes come from the first fruits of your increase and your increase may come in various forms.

Proverbs (3:9) tells us we are to, "Honour the LORD with thy substance, and with the first fruits of all thine increase." It took a little time, but I have reached a point where even if someone gives me money for a specific purpose, I tithe off that as well. Once you are familiar with the practice and understand the benefits, it becomes second nature.

People who earnestly tithe experience unique favor. Malachi admonished the people to bring all the tithes into the storehouse, that there may be meat in God's house, and God said, "Prove me … If I will not open you the windows of heaven, and pour you out a blessing, that there shall not be room enough to receive it" (3:10-11).

As an added bonus, God said He would rebuke the devourer for our sake (v11a). The devourer refers to the eater such as the locust, palmerworm, caterpillar, or any other insect prone to eat the seed and eventually the crops. The monetary seeds we sow into the

Kingdom of God will be protected by God Himself. It doesn't get any better than this. Paul asked the Romans (8:31), "What shall we then say to these things? If God be for us, who can be against us?"

I've heard people protest about tithing. They complain that it will not leave them with enough to live on. When you tithe, you must be a faith walker. If not, what you see and experience in the natural will hinder the supernatural movement of God. Once you are the recipient of a financial overflow or an unexpected windfall, you cannot squander the blessing. You cannot take the blessing and gamble it away with the mentality of easy come, easy go. You cannot manipulate the Word of God by stating, "My God shall supply all my need according to His riches in glory by Christ Jesus" (Phil 4:19). When the funds come, we have an obligation to take care of the blessing and walk with the spirit of stewardship.

Always purpose in your heart to give God your best and never give Him leftovers. The priests in the Old Testament were forbidden from offering animals to be sacrificed that were unclean and had blemishes. "And if there be any blemish therein, as if it be lame, or blind, or have any ill blemish, thou shalt not sacrifice it unto the LORD thy God" (Deu 15:21). Although we no longer present God with animal sacrifices, we should always purpose in our heart to give God our best the first time. Even when asked to give a special offering in a service, don't let fear cause you to hold back.

I've taken the time to explain tithing because it sets the stage for me to go into areas where I've experienced the benefits and favor that God bestowed upon me because of faithful tithing.

4. The First House Venture

After getting married, my husband and I moved into a garden apartment. My moving out of my grandmother's home left her alone. My grandfather had passed when I was twelve years old and it had been just the two of us ever since. After discussing the situation with my husband, we moved in with my grandmother and had the second floor of her single-family home. She didn't come upstairs often and primarily stayed on the first floor.

Although it should have helped all of us, there was constant turmoil between my husband and her. Later I found out the basis of all the friction resulted from her feeling like he had taken her baby and she couldn't forgive him for that. We all grow up but to my grandmother, I was like her change of life baby. She had raised me, so my getting married and leaving really hurt her.

After I had my first child and things were beyond tolerable, we moved out and rented a first-floor apartment in a three-family home. It was obvious that this house was once a very large one-family dwelling, now converted to a multi-dwelling structure.

The split was unusual on the first floor: the living room was very large; the room between the living room and kitchen looked like it had been part of the original dining room but someone erected a wall to make the back section a kitchen; and the kitchen was so narrow I could not stand in front of my oven and open the door. I had to stand on the side.

There wasn't much extra to be done with that makeshift kitchen and because I had a full-size washing machine and the hookups were already under the sink, I made use of the corner and put the refrigerator in the room that was between the living room and the kitchen. It was an odd look, but we made it work. The refrigerator, kitchen table, and chairs were against one wall and our baby's crib was on the opposite wall.

Our bedroom was just to the right of our baby's crib and I can only assume that room may have been the original kitchen because it had rear access to the porch and then the backyard. The bathroom looked as though it had been converted from a pantry. The one closet that existed was under the stairs to the second floor and, therefore, not very big. Taking all this into consideration you can easily see how it was once a single-family home.

We had one child at that time. The place was cold and drafty. The front door was right outside our living room door and the upstairs neighbors would never close the door all the way. During the winter months when the wind blew, the hallway would be freezing, snow would blow in from the front porch, and the living room would become frigid.

My husband had a brainchild idea and put a bell on the door that would ring if the door were left open. You cannot imagine the complaints we got because of that bell. People failed to realize that the remedy was to close the door! Needless to say, one day we came home from work and the bell was gone.

On top of that situation, literally, my upstairs neighbors had a terrible habit of throwing some of their food garbage over the back porch causing a chronic issue with stray animals. It was just one thing after another but the straw that broke the camel's back was the day, I noticed we had roaches. Oh Jesus, I don't do bugs! Years later, our family became avid campers and they quickly learned that I still didn't do bugs. One day, I became livid to see them crawling across the crib. If we sat our plates down and walked away, we were bound to attract some. I asked my neighbors if they were having an issue with bugs and they said, "A few here and there," but from what I was experiencing downstairs, I knew that could not be the truth. My grandmother taught me well how to clean house and keep it clean. I knew we weren't attracting them.

My husband was at work and called home to see how things were going. He knew how unhappy I was about those bugs. Without thinking, I sat my bowl on the coffee table for a few minutes. When I came back, roaches were swimming in the bowl. That was the final straw. Very early the next morning I packed up our baby, ran to the supermarket, and picked up about six cans of spray bombs. I drove back home, ran inside, set all the bombs, closed up the apartment, and split.

When I came home after work, the upstairs neighbors furiously met me in the driveway. They asked, "What in the [expletive] did you do?"

They had roaches all over the walls and some were falling off their ceiling. It was a mess.

I reminded them that I had inquired about the bug problem and their reply was, "A few here and there," but, truthfully, the place was infested.

In faith, I expressed to God that we needed a better place to live. He blessed us. We moved into the house next door. This time, we had a two-bedroom apartment, and once again on the first floor.

We went from a three-family to a six-family house and, yes, most likely gluttoning for punishment. Not sure if this would be better or worse because the building was owned by the same people who owned the house we had moved out of, but there was no way I could continue to live under my garbage-tossing neighbors. I did take into account that the landlords had nothing to do with the way people did or did not keep house. Collecting the monthly rent money was their priority. I, on the other hand, could no longer live under someone else's bad habits.

Having a decent relationship with the landlords made the transition from one apartment to the next easier. The property owners were brothers, and invested in and flipped houses for profit. God did bless us because, although the rent was a little more expensive, all we had to do was add the difference to the security deposit that we paid for the previous place and move in.

The apartment we vacated was left immaculate and little needed to be done in preparation for the next tenant. It sure wasn't like that when we moved in. The landlord had an exterminator take care of the entire house and shortly thereafter they were able to rent the vacated apartment without losing any rent revenue.

In your endeavor to excel, whether it's spiritually, physically, or financially, always be in remembrance, "For with God nothing shall be impossible" (Luke 1:37). Put your faith in action and allow God to do the rest. Never let the adversary fool you into believing that you can circumvent the process and get the same results that you would if you stepped aside and let God be God.

After a few months in the new apartment, the winter months were upon us and we found ourselves running into a similar issue experienced in the old place. The primary entrance to the common hallway was outside our kitchen door this time. Various occupants would leave the front door open and all that cold air had free access to come in.

The landlord controlled the one furnace that supplied heat to the entire building, but the furnace wasn't sufficient enough to provide basic heat. The house wasn't insulated, and the windows were excessively drafty. There wasn't a way to maintain a decent temperature even by running electric heaters. Mind you, I wasn't looking for tropical temperatures inside, just to not be required to dress like I would have if going outside.

If the outside temperature wasn't freezing, I could let my son sleep in his room, and heat from the kitchen would offset the cold. When it was terribly cold outside, he slept in the living room, and I would close off his bedroom from the rest of the apartment. One morning when I went into his room to get his clothes for school, I could see my breath, indicating that room had absolutely no heat. Believe me, that was no way to live.

After receiving numerous complaints from the tenants, the landlord decided to remove the old furnace and install separate units. Now, each tenant held the responsibility to pay for his or her own heat and hot water. When questioned about adjusting down the rent, the landlord said there would be no adjustments, as he needed to be compensated for what he spent to install the new furnaces. This modification became a double-edged sword because of the drafty windows and that darn door people failed to keep closed. Our gas bill skyrocketed. By then we had two children and that arrangement wasn't working. There was no way we could endure another winter there.

My husband suggested putting a bell on the door.

I said, "I don't think that would be a good idea. It didn't work next door with two other families. I can't imagine the flack we'd catch from the five who live in this house."

He didn't agree but, for the sake of not causing a rift with the other tenants, he dropped the idea of installing a bell.

After explaining the situation to my pastor, she asked, "Have you considered buying a house?"

I told her we didn't have the money to purchase a house and definitely not enough for a decent down payment.

She asked, "Have you considered purchasing a HUD home?"

We were not familiar with that process but had a willingness to look into it. You never know what kind of blessing God has in store for you.

By faith, I began looking into HUD properties and where I could obtain funds to make a move. After seeking the face of God, I located a two-family home in a nearby county. It was a HUD house that had been abandoned for more than two years. Vandals had removed all the copper piping and it was in need of a good cleaning but otherwise would not take a lot of money to make habitable. We figured we could rent out the first floor giving us an income to help pay the mortgage. The ultimate goal was to save enough thereafter to buy a single-family dwelling for ourselves and then rent the second and third floors where we would have stayed.

After taking several thorough looks at the interior of the property and driving through the neighborhood at different times to observe the atmosphere on and off peak, we decided to make an offer. The starting bid was $11,500. Under the direction of my pastor, who in times past had purchased HUD properties as rental investments for the ministry, we offered $12,000.

On the day the bids were to be opened we found out that another family outbid us. During the hold period they had to come up with 10% of their bid in order to lock down the deal. The holding period expired which meant we could then submit our $1,200 down payment. Unbeknownst to us as we were about to leave with the realtor to go to the HUD office, he received a call that the first bidder had obtained an extension. The realtor said, "In all my years of dealing with HUD I've never known them to give anyone an extension; these homes are sold on the basis that if you cannot come up with the 10%, the property is immediately offered to the next highest bidder."

We then had to wait another two weeks to see if that first bidder was able to produce the required funds. I was disappointed because we really liked this house. It had potential and a big yard for the kids. It was suggested to me to start looking at other properties. I did out of obedience to show I had a contingency plan. I expressed to God, "Lord, I know this house is for us."

After the two-week waiting period the realtor called and informed us the first bidder still could not get their money together. HUD will not give them another extension and wanted to close the books on the property. He had informed the HUD agent that his clients had the funds in hand and were ready to move forward.

We immediately made our way to the HUD office and closed the deal. My faith in God kept me encouraged as I saw one opportunity after another open up. Initially, things looked bleak, but as time went on, all the pieces fell into place. Once again, walk by faith and not by sight. Remember, what God has for you is for you.

5. Life of a Furnace Extended

I had spoken to my dad about the plumbing work that needed to be done in the new house. Although many years prior my dad had moved to the mid-west, he remained friends with a gentleman in my immediate area who just happened to be a plumber.

I reached out to Mr. Ross, who came over to give an estimate on the required plumbing work. It wasn't as bad as we thought it would be because everything was dry when the pipes were removed. The walls had not been damaged in the process of vandals extracting the copper pipes. It was just a matter of re-snaking the pipes and soldering them into place. The boiler was old but still functional. It was originally a coal burner that had been converted to oil. I remembered as a little girl in my grandparent's home being around when coal was delivered. I recognized a similar coal bin that existed in this house with a nearby window under the stairs for the coal shoot.

After moving in and being able to fully explore the layout of the home, we could tell the house was once a one-family dwelling and had been renovated into a multi-family dwelling. In years past, big homes were not unusual because couples had large families and it didn't cost as much to heat the home. We were into the year 1983 and oil was expensive. I remember in one case, to save money we opted for a cheaper grade of oil, and it stunk up the entire house beyond belief. Lord, I was so glad we didn't fill the tank. It took weeks to get rid of that bad batch of oil because we spent our money to buy it and didn't want to run the heat excessively high and create a need to once again replenish our supply.

As time went on, we came to realize the one boiler didn't have the capability to adequately heat the home. The first floor was very comfortable; so much so, that our tenant let her children run around in their undies in the dead of winter while we would freeze on the second and third floors.

Our bathroom had no steam radiator. We depended upon heat from the riser that went through the bathroom ceiling and extended to the 3rd floor. We had to place foam insulation at the bottom of the riser so that no one would bump into a hot pipe, especially in the middle of the night. The downside was that this insulation obstructed some of the heat, so we needed a better remedy.

We managed to make it through a couple of winters but knew it would eventually be time to replace the old boiler. When you have a dedicated prayer life, the effectiveness of your prayers will unfold favor on your behalf sometimes before you ask. I reached out to Mr. Ross once again and he returned with a crew to replace the old boiler. Since he had previously worked on that unit, he was familiar with how many BTU's was needed. God used him to be a double blessing to us; the cost of the new unit wasn't as much as we originally thought and once he added in the cost of installation, it was still within our budget.

As the men dismantled the boiler, Mr. Ross called me to the basement because they didn't believe what they were seeing. He showed me how the pieces were literally disintegrating in their hands and they asked, "Did you run this boiler last winter?"

My answer was, "Yes, and basically since Mr. Ross fired it up the first time."

We were operating under prayer. Remember I said previously that the house had been vacant for two years. The boiler sat for the same length of time.

He said that based upon the present condition of the boiler it should not have functioned beyond the first winter and he didn't understand how it did.

I let him know that I had great trust in the Lord, and God knew at that time we didn't have the funds to replace the boiler, so God preserved it and kept us safe. Faith was the evidence of what we could not have seen months prior.

On a couple of occasions, it choked up. I went to the basement and laid hands on it, in the name of Jesus. Things appear to go dreadfully wrong when the weather is extremely bad and it could be almost impossible to get someone to come out for a service call, but if you call on Jesus, He'll answer prayer. So, for the duration of the winter months, God preserved the life of that old boiler and we didn't experience one incident that could have resulted in a fire or catastrophe.

6. An Angel on Assignment

Some of these stories may seem unbelievable to you unless you've experienced similar events or, on some level, can relate to them.

We were attending Roselle Christian Church under the now late Reverend Mother Derris Cargile. Most Sundays we would leave the house early to attend Sunday school and stay for the balance of the day. Each Sunday it was customary to serve dinner after morning service allowing us to remain at the church for the afternoon service. Nowadays, you find people want to put God on a clock, get in and get out, and not give God an opportunity to let His presence truly saturate the service, provide deliverance, and change people's lives.

After I got married and had children of my own, they too attended our all-day services. The ministry gave them a good foundation. Proverbs (22:6) encourages us to, "Train up a child in the way he should go: and when he is old, he will not depart from it." Now, those of you who are parents and have imparted this Scripture into the lives of your children are all too aware of what happens when some of our children reach those adolescent years. You put your faith on high alert and trust God that they will not depart the solid teaching you've instilled in them. Our offspring may get sidetracked but maintain your faith in God to keep them from getting sideswiped and unable to recover from the hit.

Anyway, one particular Sunday we left church and headed for home, getting off the highway onto a local street, we drove west onto another main street that put us a block from home. I was driving an old Buick station wagon that had chronic issues. The car decided to stall in a bad location. There was nowhere to pull over. I had four very tired kids in the car, no cell phone, and no other way to call for help.

The Holy Spirit said, "Put the car in neutral," and I did.

The car had power steering and power breaks, so I had no idea what to expect. The car slowly began to coast down the street. I figured going downhill I would continue to coast until I could safely pull the car over. From there the kids and I would then get out and walk home because we would be safe and close enough to do so.

There are times you think you have things figured out but when God is in control it's a reminder that our ways are not like His ways (Isaiah 55:8). We should never become anxious in trying to plan the next move but when things are spontaneously occurring, let God be in full control.

As we slowly coasted to the corner, I knew it would be tricky from there because I needed to make a left turn onto the street that ran perpendicular to my block. Don't you know as I approached the corner the light turned red? I had to come to a complete stop putting both feet on the brake. All I could do was sigh. While I sat, I tried to start the car and it was dead. At that point I said, "Lord, I'm going to have faith and trust in you to get us through this. I don't believe you will leave me stranded with small children in the car at one of the worst intersections in the area."

The light turned green and there were cars behind me. As soon as the light changes to green, impatient drivers behind you want you to immediately proceed. In some cases, it's not a good thing to instantly move out into the intersection. I've seen where drivers going in the opposite direction ran the amber and, subsequently, the red light causing a collision.

In this situation it took crazy faith, the kind of faith exhibited by the men who removed part of the roof where Jesus was ministering and lowered a sick man through the opening (Matt 9:2-8). Can you say that you have that kind of faith? Is your faith being strengthened from reading my experiences?

The Holy Spirit instructed me to take my foot off the brake. Out of obedience, I did. The car in front of me pulled off and then my car began to slowly roll as though someone was pushing it. It continuously rolled forward, although the car was still in a stalled state. I was able to turn the steering wheel to the left and roll through the intersection. Next, we were headed to a moderate incline and I knew things would become interesting. The car continued to roll. It was smooth and steady. I maneuvered the incline and then made a right onto my street. The car rolled down the street, cleared the dip under the railroad tracks, rolled up another incline, and stopped right in front of our house.

I still believe to this day, after I prayed while stranded, God sent an angel and that angel pushed us home. There is no other explanation for that phenomenon. Once the car was officially in Park, we all got out of it giving God praise for what He had just done. The kids may have been initially tired from the long day, but everyone's energy level had been renewed.

Therefore, it is important for parents to live a life that is exemplary of Christ. When our children see and experience faith in action, it gives integrity to the Word of God and teaches them to trust in Him on a whole new level.

When children get excited about the goodness of the Lord, adults tend to see their relationship with Him just a little differently. My husband was trying to get a few last minutes of sleep before preparing for work, but there was no way that was going to happen that night. When God works a miracle for you, you cannot help but to be encouraged. His Word remains true, when He says He will never leave nor forsake you (Heb 13:5). Do you feel the same?

We had a second incident with the problematic station wagon. We were camping out of state. It was a Sunday morning and I was packing for the return trip home. We owned the trailer and had a storage agreement, meaning we could leave the unit onsite for the season. That made life easier because I could leave some items inside the trailer and transport only the perishable food. The children were playing, and their dad was loading the station wagon. As I finished, he decided to start the car to let it run a few minutes before we got on the highway.

He turned the key in the ignition, and nothing happened, not even a click.

I said to myself, Oh, this is not good.

Both of us had to be back to work on Monday, the kids needed to be back in school, and who could rescue us on a Sunday?

I told him to, "Open the hood," but by then he was angry and when he got angry, he was not cooperative on any level.

We came to realize how temperamental that car was. It had a tendency to malfunction at some of the most inopportune times. I stopped what I was doing, went outside, laid hands on the car by faith in the name of Jesus, and said a short prayer.

As I went back inside like all of that was second nature to me, he looked at me as though I had just lost my mind. You would have thought that after all the years we had been married he would have been used to it, but he wasn't.

After about ten minutes, I told him, "Go try to start the car."

He retorted, "Why? When this happens it just doesn't start."

I had to really persuade him to give it a try. I truly believed the Spirit of God had touched the car and it would start.

I guess just to humor me he got in the car, turned the key, and from the trailer I said once again, "In the name of Jesus."

The car started. I was so ecstatic I jumped out of the trailer to give God praise. You can take a quick praise break, even when in the Pennsylvania woods.

Without hesitation, we gathered the kids together, everyone got in the car, I locked the trailer, and we drove straight home without any more incidents from that car.

On Monday, the station wagon was taken to the mechanic, who could find no reason why the vehicle would not start, but one thing was certain, James 5:16b (TLB) says, "The earnest prayer of a righteous man has great power and wonderful results." We all experienced a wonderful result the day before and it gave us yet one more opportunity to give God praise for what He had done for us.

7. Round Trip on 1/8 Tank of Gas

At this point of my career, I was working for a telecommunications company that chronically moved our department from one location to another. Competition was fierce and promotions were difficult to achieve. Being a large corporation, in a lot of cases it wasn't what you knew, but whom you knew. Politics were prevalent. Some of us, as lower-level managers, saw elevation where the qualifications nowhere met the required competencies that were needed to properly fulfill the position. The level of frustration was through the roof and morale was at an all-time low as qualified employees kept being overlooked.

Our team was subjected to yet another move, except this relocation resulted in a lengthy daily commute. I'm talking about 46 miles one way. Depending upon the traffic, if I made it to the office within an hour, I was doing well. Working from home had not yet been offered, nor was flex time an option, so we had to be onsite and at our desk in order to be considered on time.

I have never been fond of clutter. My infamous cliché is, "When in doubt, throw it out." When it came time to move, I had maybe 3 file-size boxes that contained my personal and office supplies. On the first day at our new location, we were given time to set up at our new work areas. All I pulled out of my boxes were a couple of ink pens, some post-it pads, a stapler with the remover, and correction tape. I was serious when I said, "I'm here, but I don't plan to remain long."

The main issue with that new location came down to my personal finances. We were sent so far away from our homes, and no one provided any kind of compensation to cover the additional gas we were consuming and the tolls we had to pay to get there. I tried to economize as much as possible, but things were tough.

Each day, I would pray before pulling out of the driveway. The highway was scary. There were so many cars and motorists drove like maniacs. You know how it is to drive in unfamiliar territory; you appear to get in the way of everyone else who's accustomed to the traffic and the pace.

I also had to cross a large bridge that was terrifying especially when returning home at the end of the day. All I could see were brake lights in front of me and headlights on the opposite side of the road. That added to the stress created by the commute.

In my position, I only got paid once a month. If I didn't budget well, I ran out of money before I ran out of month. Sometimes, the best-laid plans experience a hiccup. I had to trust God on a level which I had never trusted Him before. Aside from asking for traveling mercy, I also needed to keep an adequate amount of gas in the car. This newer vehicle, unlike that station wagon, was dependable but not very energy efficient. On cold days, I would bundle myself with extra garments and cover my knees with a blanket so that I could reduce fuel consumption and not run the heat for the entire trip but that did not always work. If it snowed or there was freezing rain, I needed heat to keep the windshield clear.

One day in particular, I made it home with maybe 1/8 of a tank of gas remaining in the car. I didn't go out that night because I knew I had to be back on the highway the next morning. Driving those miles was tiring and on top of all that madness, I had children to care for once I arrived home.

The next morning, I got in the car, prayed as usual, and conveyed to God, "I'm going to trust you today like none other. Under normal circumstances the remaining gas would barely get me to work, nonetheless provide me with enough for a round trip, but I trust you."

I didn't have any money that could be used to put gas in the car, not even spare loose change, which I had used occasionally. We didn't have EZ Pass at that time and I still had to pay the tolls.

I left the house, got on the highway, and drove to work. The Holy Spirit advised me to not focus on the gas gauge and to just drive. So that is what I did.

When I got to work, only then did I look at the gas gauge, and it still read 1/8 of a tank. I was like, "Wow!"

Then I said, "Thank you, Lord. You made sure I got to work, and I believe you'll make sure that I get home."

When my workday ended, I got back in the car, thanked God for traveling mercy, and headed home. Once again ignoring what the gas gauge read, I trusted God.

I arrived home safe and sound. Once I parked the car, I looked at the gauge and only then did it hit the, "E."

I sat in awe of what God had done for me and when I finally went inside the house, there was a blessing waiting for me. My tenant, who ran late with her rent, paid me in cash. I deducted tithe money from what she gave me, as I always did when I received the rent, and was able to take the car and fill the tank.

God wants us to get to a level where we trust Him without reservation; "God is faithful to the faithful" (Elder Hailey cliché). Take the limits off your Heavenly Father.

8. Faith that Canceled Debt

I have had experiences where God has literally canceled debt. In many cases, with the wonderful world of technology, once you owe a bill you are required to pay it off. Normally, debt doesn't fall off the database.

Decades ago, my husband had back surgery and, based upon the procedure, the insurance company had established perimeters contingent upon no complications, and they used that to determine surgeon compensation. The surgeon charged Three Thousand Dollars ($3,000.00) more than what the insurance company considered reasonable and customary for that procedure.

The surgeon stated that he had to perform a few extra actions that were itemized in his bill and although the insurance company rejected his rationale for the extras, those charges would still need to be covered. In such a case, the patient is responsible for the outstanding balance.

I told the surgeon, "We're now down to one income while my husband recovers and have children to feed and a mortgage to pay. The budget is already tight and there's nothing extra to pay toward a bill of this magnitude."

I also told him, "The best I can do is squeeze out about $50 each month, but even that would stretch our finances."

A month after the surgery I began making payments on the specified days as promised. After doing that for a ridiculous period of time, I went to the Lord because I was in an uncomfortable position. If I paid bills I didn't have enough for groceries, and if I purchased food, there wasn't enough to pay the bills.

I said to the Lord, "I need to approach this doctor again regarding the remaining balance on this bill and I'm going to believe that the remaining balance will be canceled."

One day, as I sat at the table and looked at the bill I prayed, "Lord, this doctor charged more than he should have, leaving us with no recourse but to pay what the insurance company refused to cover. What should I do now?"

The Lord advised me to write the check for the usual amount and include a note stating that since the surgery I had paid on the bill as promised; and inquire if the bill could be considered *paid in full* with the enclosed check. Despite the condition of my finances, I still pulled God's tithe money out of any monetary increase I received, trusting God to extend what remained.

I mailed the check and the note along with my other bills. A few days later, as I was sitting under the hair dryer, the phone rang but I could not get to it, so I asked my daughter to answer the call.

She said, "Mom, it's the doctor's office and the lady said you don't owe any more money on the bill."

I jumped out from under the hair dryer and started giving God praise. I was so happy and grateful for what had transpired. When you have an experience like this it encourages you to maintain faith when similar situations occur. Faith and obedience working together gave me the victory over the remaining amount. Yes, the balance was canceled.

Well, I had another medical bill on which I conscientiously made monthly payments. That bill included charges for two separate procedure codes for services rendered on the same day. For some unknown reason, the doctor's office sent one of the charges to collections. When I called the medical office, the billing manager was apologetic because it had been a human error but stated once the bill goes to collections, there was nothing they could do to change the coding. I was furious because in some instances when a bill is sent to collections, it looks like negligence on the part of the patient, and could negatively affect the credit score. I had to clear it up quickly.

After that call, I was too angry to speak to anyone else and decided to wait until the next day and call the collection agency. It turned out to be a blessing in disguise because I had an opportunity to get past my frustration and remember to once again exercise faith. Sometimes we allow our emotions to take control and, honestly, that is where I was that day.

God canceled debt for me before and knowing nothing shall be impossible unto Him (Luke 1:37), He could do it again. And, actually I had the upper hand because I had proof that I had been consistently paying on the bill.

The next day, I called the collection agency and had a conversation with one of their representatives. Much to my surprise, she was a very pleasant woman. I explained the situation and stated that each month I had diligently paid on the account. I could not understand how part of the bill was sent to collections; yet, the doctor's office retained the other portion of the bill for services rendered on the same day.

I asked her about the remaining balance because I wanted to make sure that no hidden charges were being added. The agent told me the amount they were given, but suggested I give her a call on the next business day because their reports were due to run that evening and the numbers would definitely be accurate. She was also kind enough to give me her extension, which rarely happened, so that I would not have to go through the 1-800-#, and explain the situation to another representative. The favor of God was in action.

That night, before I went to bed, I prayed to God that He would once again show favor to me regarding the bill. I also acknowledged that down through the years He had been immensely gracious to our family, "Lord, please do it one more time."

The following day, I called and spoke directly with the representative with whom I had spoken previously. Considering that her office interacts with a lot of people, I reminded her of our conversation because I wasn't sure if she remembered me.

Ironically, she did remember and asked for the reference number. I gave her the number, she pulled up the account, and I heard her say, "Where is the balance?"

I asked her to clarify. "Did the report run last night?"

She said, "Yes, and for some odd reason your remaining balance is zero!"

All I could say was, "Thank you, Lord."

I was so excited until I heard the Holy Spirit say, "Wait a minute."

At that point my instruction was, "Ask for a copy of the report," so I asked the agent to fax me a copy for my records.

She immediately faxed the report and, sure enough, at the bottom of the page it stated, "Balance due, zero."

With a monumental outcome, God made me so happy that day. He has shown up in miraculous ways that still bring tears to my eyes. I've learned to be more than grateful to God for all His benefits toward me.

9. Faith to Stand for Another

Faith being, "the evidence of things not seen" (Heb 11:1), manifested a healing through believing and obedience. My cousin and his wife had five small children. In 1993, they were renting a nice home that comfortably accommodated a family of their size, but found, as time went on, the landlord became a very unpleasant person to deal with and started demanding that they move.

My cousin worked a lot of hours as a firefighter, and very often his wife was home alone with their children. Subsequently, he wasn't always available to leave his station, run home to resolve issues with the landlord, and return back to work. When on call, he did not have the flexibility to do that, and the last thing he wanted was to jeopardize his career.

Knowing it was inevitable that they would have to move, they began looking for another residence. Not in a position to pay a down payment to purchase a house meant they would have to find another place to rent. Landlords can be very particular about selecting tenants. Couples with more than two children may face challenges; you cannot imagine the obstacles for a family of seven.

As my cousin continued to work his full-time job, he also picked up a few extra hours here and there to help build enough finances to make the move. His wife was into arts and crafts and did what she could to earn a little extra money working from home.

They were ambitious in their search, but the landlord turned up the heat on his demand that they move.

The stress became too great for my cousin's wife to bear and she suffered a mild stroke. I believe his motive was money because the house was in a nice area and he could rent it for more than what he was getting from them. The love of money being the root of all evil (1 Tim 6:10), made a bad situation worst.

When the call was received that my cousins' wife had suffered a stroke, I was very upset and asked the Lord what I should do. As I waited for an answer from the Lord, when I could I would go by and help tidy up, and my husband would make sure they had groceries. We, ourselves, were a family of six, so first-hand experience made it possible to know what it took to keep the ship running, but at times not necessarily smoothly.

Prior to the stroke, my cousin's wife was making calls trying to set up appointments to view other places to live, and trying to coordinate onsite visits when her husband was not working because she didn't drive. After the stroke, she still tried to make calls because the mandate remained in force, whereas, they needed to move; but her terrible stutter made communication difficult and because some people thought she was a prank caller they would hang up on her.

One morning, while I was in prayer, I asked the Lord again what else I could do to help. "Lord, I've trusted you to help me through many of my own situations. Faith led me through each and every one of them. Now, I'm asking on behalf of someone else."

When you pray, you cannot forget that prayer is a dialogue, not a monologue. It's not you doing all the talking, but you have to give God an opportunity to speak. When you approach God on critical matters, it's always best to have adequate time to pray so you can allow God to speak. Sometimes, people look for a quick fix when all God wants is quality time, and to not be treated like a timeshare. I was instructed to anoint her with oil and pray for her, in the name of Jesus.

Previously, I've prayed for people when it was just God and me, but I had never prayed for anyone while laying hands on them. When laying hands, one must be careful because spirits get transferred. That's why 1 Timothy (5:22) cautions us to, "Lay hands suddenly on no man."

I wanted to be obedient and especially after seeing the end result of previous prayers, so I started making preparation for the trip. I set aside a specific time to pray for this assignment and committed to fast from 6 AM to 12 noon, a few days before going over to pray. I also evoked the Holy Spirit to give me the Scriptures that would be appropriate.

That evening, I went to my cousin's home and he was at work, but his wife was there with a long-time friend of hers, who was also led to stop by and lend a hand with their children. We know how children can be, you can give them instructions, but at times if you're not able to physically make sure they do what you've asked, the task may not get completely accomplished.

The Lord led me to minister to her first and explain what I was told to do in accordance with the instructions God had given to me. Although she wasn't currently active in the church, she grew up in ministry and had experience with the Lord. She had respect for me being sent to be a blessing to her.

As I ministered, I could tell she was receptive to what was being said. God had prepared her heart to receive what was about to happen. As we've been taught, we may come in contact with people who may never step foot in a church and the only ministry they may experience is through us. This is why our lives must exhibit Christ and we must be genuine in all things that pertain to Him.

As we proceeded, I realized the house had become quiet. With five children at home, it was remarkable. God settled down the atmosphere because He wanted to be heard. I quoted several healing Scriptures and then poured a touch of oil on top of her head in the name of Jesus. I said a prayer as led by the Holy Spirit and told her she should see results a little at a time. I admonished her to give God thanks for every improvement she experienced and to not postpone the praise, but to do it as soon as she realized it.

ROBIN M. HAILEY

A few weeks later, unbeknownst to me, my husband was talking to my cousin's wife on the phone and during the conversation she had a quick question. Because I was at work, he had to conference me. For the first few seconds, I wasn't sure who I was talking to and then I realized it was she. The awful stutter that she acquired as a result of the stroke was completely gone.

As we spoke to each other, she informed me that she could walk without dragging her leg and had full use of both her hands. Her speech was as steady as it had been before the stroke. The doctors were confounded by her recovery. I was at work and tried to contain myself, but it was difficult.

When you experience the goodness of the Lord in the land of the living (Psa 27:13) you want to be spontaneous in your response to God. If you procrastinate when it comes to giving God praise, you may forget. God inhabits the praises of His people (Psa 22:3). We are encouraged to praise Him, "Praise him for his mighty acts: praise him according to his excellent greatness," (Psa 150:2). Our unprompted praise shows God our gratitude.

Have you ever been at work and had to leave your desk and make a quick trip outside or go to the restroom, to get out of the mainstream of your co-workers and take a praise break? I didn't want to do anything that would be considered out of order and, although my co-workers knew I had a love for the Lord, everything should be decent and in order (1 Cor 14:40). I shared a work area with someone, but at that particular time I was in the office alone, so I got up, cut a few steps in the name of Jesus, and sat back down. Nehemiah (8:10) reminds us that, "The joy of the Lord is your strength," and every time you exhibit joy in the Lord you acquire strength. Your praise shows the devil that regardless of how things look, you believe the report of the Lord.

My cousin's healing restored her independency. I reminded her that she's required to give God praise every day for the healing. Never forget nor minimize what He has done but take it personally. "My help cometh from the Lord, which made heaven and earth," (Psa 121:2).

Our obligation is to remember that without Him, we are nothing. God is very deserving of our praise and only He should get the credit for the miracles that occur. I stepped out on faith on her behalf and by my obedience in following God's directive, the evidence was the manifestation of my cousin's healing.

Faith to Believe Healing

There were many young people in the ministry of which I got saved. I watched them grow into adolescents and then adults who married and had children of their own. There was one young lady in particular; her grandmother was the pastor of the ministry and her mother was one of the vocalists and musicians. In essence, it was a family church with a solid foundation and very closely knit.

Around 1991, after getting married this young lady became pregnant but she began having unusual symptoms and spent days in bed unable to get much of anything accomplished. One day, I was in prayer and was led to pray for her specifically. Just as clear as day, I heard the Lord give me the strangest instruction. He told me to get seven Life Savor peppermints and set them aside to be prayed over. Now, you know I had to have faith to do this and then follow the subsequent instructions. At the end of the prayer, still under the unction of the Holy Spirit, I was further instructed to give the peppermints to her and tell her each morning when she got up to eat one.

Afterward, I sat on the side of the bed and pondered those instructions. Once again, I put more thought into it than I should have. I had never heard of anything like that before nor heard where anyone else had been given those instructions. To be honest I was afraid: *What happens if it doesn't work? How will people perceive me if it fails?*

Doubt was running rampant in my mind and spirit. I was being pulled out of my comfort zone once again and lost sight that God wanted to use me to be a blessing to a pregnant woman who could not take any kind of medication.

I purchased a bag of individually wrapped Life Savers peppermints and set the seven aside. The first opportunity I had to talk without being overheard, I called her grandmother who, like I've said, was our pastor. I told her the instructions God gave me. She supported me 100% and said, "Go do as you were told by the Lord."

This Woman of God had prophecy on her life, but she flowed in a subtle way. I know that she believed that I had heard from the Lord, otherwise she would have discouraged me from doing it. Assured that it was the will of God, I prayed over the peppermints in the name of Jesus and gave them to the mother-to-be with the instructions God had given to me.

Glory to God! By the 7th day, she was feeling better. Her quality of life had been restored and whatever was causing her to feel so ill was gone. I cannot imagine what she was going through being pregnant for the first time and feeling so miserable, but the power of God in the name of Jesus worked and kept trauma away from her unborn baby. I encourage you to step out on faith and trust God even when the instructions bring doubt and fear.

This act of faith was a blessing to her, but it also blessed me, and I had to repent to God for my initial doubt.

Faith to Pray for My Doctor

In 2011, I was in the hospital during my return stay for the closing of the fasciotomies in my leg. One morning, the plastic surgeon who performed the procedure came to my room to remove some of the staples from the healing wounds. He was noticeably walking kind of bent over and I asked, "What happened to you?"

I could tell he was in a lot of pain, he said that when he was putting on his socks, he turned the wrong way, and developed a terrible pain in his back.

I told him that I had done something similar one day trying to put on my pantyhose in a rush. I'd had a job interview, as well as a good distance to drive, and didn't want to be late. When that occurred, I could hardly walk, and the pain was excruciating. I still went on the interview although I did not get the position. It was difficult to camouflage the pain I was in and undoubtedly the interviewing manager could tell I was distracted, but I appreciated the opportunity to speak with her.

During my weeks of inpatient care and trips for surgery, before they administered the anesthesia and proceeded with each surgical procedure, the doctor respected my request to pray. I figured that being hospitalized three months and enduring eight surgical procedures, somebody in the operating room needed to be praying. It was never a long prayer, just a few words asking the God of Abraham, Isaac, and Jacob, to oversee all procedures that were required. I worded my prayers in that fashion because the doctors and most of the attendants were Jewish and I wanted them to experience firsthand my faith in the true and living God.

With that being said, because the doctor with the back spasm could not bend over, he had his attendant remove some of my staples. As she was working, in my spirit I was talking to the Lord asking if it would be appropriate for me to pray for the doctor.

God answered a question with a question. (Don't you hate when people do that?)

God's question was "Why would you not?"

I replied that I believed although I was bedridden, I had faith that my doctor would get healed.

After his attendant was finished, the doctor made sure everything else was fine, she re-wrapped my leg, and they proceeded to leave. Before he got to the door, I called his name and said, "You know how much I believe in the power of prayer and the results that can be achieved."

He said, "Yes."

I then asked if he would allow me to anoint his back and pray for him, and much to my surprise, he said, "Yes."

I understood the discomfort he was in and yet he was trying to make his rounds, so that prayer had to be short yet powerful. It's not always the length of your prayer that matters; it boils down to the quality of your prayer. Knowing he was devoutly Jewish I had to think quickly, "Lord, should I say in the name of the God of Abraham, Isaac, and Jacob; or in the name of Jesus?"

The answer was a no brainer, "In the name of Jesus," because Jesus grew up Jewish.

It was in the name of Jesus that I prayed and after the prayer he left the room. I could tell he was still in pain by the way he walked but, my expectation was that he would be relieved from what he was going through.

The next day the doctor came to check my leg and didn't need his assistant.

I said, "Oh my, you're walking much better today."

He began doing a little dance. He let me know that after he left my room, the pain started to subside and within a matter of hours it was gone all together and he was slowly able to straighten up.

I thank God that I didn't let hesitation, nor my circumstance, hinder me in being a blessing to someone who was doing all they could to help save my leg. Doctors can treat you but, in the end, God does the healing. Let God use you for His glory.

10. When God Speaks

Second Chronicles (20:15) reminds us that, "the battle is not yours, but God's." A battle can be physical or spiritual. Sometimes, it appears that the physical battles are easier to win than the spiritual ones. If God's Word tells us that the battle is not ours, we should rest assured to know that it has already been won. Sometimes you must do like Moses told the children of Israel when the Egyptian army was on right behind them, "Fear ye not, stand still, and see the salvation of the Lord," (Exo 14:13).

Endurance can be challenged from many different directions and make us feel defeated and worn. To endure means you have the ability to withstand hardship or adversity; especially during a prolonged or stressful situation. A portion of Matthew (24:13) reminds us that only those who endure to the end shall be saved. If you manage to endure, you will not be overtaken by the situation.

When my mother became dreadfully ill, I had to exercise endurance that lasted more than three months. Here we go with another three-month period. Before being hospitalized she had gone back and forth to the doctor suffering from a fever that mysteriously afflicted her body and lingered. Each time the fever flared up it would weaken her the more, leaving her with no appetite, causing her to lose weight, and sometimes become incoherent. Due to the frequency of the flare-ups, she didn't always have adequate time to recuperate from one episode to the next.

One day, I made fresh raisin bread and had planned to take Mom a few slices, but a situation occurred in my household and I could not leave. The next day, after work my sister stopped by to check on Mom, who lived alone. Upon entering the house my sister called out to her but received no response. She went straight to the bedroom and found Mom lying on the floor next to the bed. Evidently, Mom got up sometime during the evening to get Jell-O out of the fridge and when she got back to the bedroom, she collapsed.

Nowadays, seniors have medical alert devices. If in distress they can press a button for help, but if no movement is detected for a period of time, help is dispatched. If Mom had one at that time, she would not have laid on the floor all night. When I was contacted, I felt absolutely terrible because if I had gone by the evening before, that would have been avoided. She was rushed to the hospital where they immediately began to hydrate her in an attempt to improve her condition.

Mom spent more than two months in a local hospital. The source of the fever was still unknown, and her chart was labeled, "FUO," which is the acronym for Fever of Unknown Origin.

The doctors asked a variety of questions: Had she traveled abroad; Who she had been in contact with; Were there any other family members suffering from this illness or had they experienced these symptoms?

The answer to all their questions was always, "No."

She didn't travel far and hardly left the county in which she lived. Trying to pinpoint a source was becoming increasingly impossible.

The doctors checked to see if she had possibly been bitten by an insect that could have caused the symptoms, but all possible tests came back negative. In the meantime, things were becoming critical, because of the fever and her poor appetite her body began breaking down due to lack of protein and she developed massive bedsores.

She was in chronic pain all over like the pain I've heard people experience with Fibromyalgia. Although the doctor prescribed a pain management regiment, when the staff tried to reposition her, her facial expressions gave a clear indication of how much discomfort she was actually in.

My faith in God kept me praying and believing that, regardless of how worse things appeared to be, she would get healed and be released from the hospital. Near the end of almost two months, the doctor's being very mystified in dealing with the illness, asked permission to send tissue samples to the National Center for Disease Control in Bethesda, Maryland. The NCDC had all the newly developed, high technical equipment and processes. The doctors figured approaching the mystery from a national level should bring answers to such a puzzling illness.

The samples were expedited to Maryland and after a few days a response from them rendered no tangible answers. They were as confounded as the staff here in the local hospital. After this disappointment, the doctors stated there was nothing further they could do for her. That is something family members never want to hear.

Basically, we were told the only option left was to make her comfortable until the end. How does someone with unwavering faith in God accept the possible reality that a family member is terminally ill? Was I being compelled to accept such a diagnosis? The doctors were admitting defeat; did they expect my sister and me to do likewise?

Up to that point God had still been silent to our prayers and His final decision. I didn't want to misinterpret His silence and put my own spin on what God's response would be.

With so much riding on making the best decision, we started asking around to see if another doctor or hospital would be willing to pick up her case. Physically, she was in such bad shape, we

ROBIN M. HAILEY

knew it would be nearly impossible to find anyone who would be willing to take on such a massive responsibility.

In an effort to seek alternatives, utilizing a small network of people, we found a doctor who was willing to take her on as a patient even after hearing about the complexity of her condition. It was our understanding that he had experience in dealing with unexplainable fevers and was interested in the new challenge. His acceptance was God-sent because at that time people's perception was that my sister and I were not doing all that was possible to push for an answer.

At that point I believe the local hospital was just about tired of all of the family and friends who inquired about her status. Sometimes, tempers flared, and words were hostile, and when the doctor saw one of us coming down the hall he would turn and go the other way just to avoid being asked questions for which he had no answers.

I came to realize after doing my own research that a significant percentage of FUO cases are caused by miscellaneous conditions, and there is no standard set of rules for evaluating and, subsequently, treating them. Each case had to be approached as though it was the first of its kind before recommendations could be made to proceed with treatment. Current inquiries showed that steps had been established as guidelines and, according to the symptoms, a plan of action could be developed.

Authorization was obtained from the insurance company to move Mom to another hospital in a different county and we started the medical investigative process all over again. My sister and I were the only children my Mom had, and it was difficult for both of us to assure the family that all was being done to understand Mom's illness and make sure she was getting the best care.

One of our concerns was to actively minimize Mom's suffering and make sure her pain was being managed. I kept praying, believing God, and exhibiting a positive attitude through that entire ordeal, maintaining unwavering faith that the situation would not end in heartbreak.

Mom had been so sick for what appeared to be an eternity; she hardly spoke half dozen words in the three months she was hospitalized. The fever had racked her body and depleted her physically, but not spiritually. When we prayed, she would respond by sometimes opening her eyes as to acknowledge that she was right there with us, and when we quoted a Scripture that was one of her favorites, she would raise her hand and gently wave it.

That was a testimony to us that regardless what you go through, you can always look to God, the author and finisher of your faith (Heb 12:2). Some people find it difficult to maintain a positive attitude when going through life's storms, but God has a way of making us strong when we are weak (2 Cor 12:10). We persevere because of the strength we gain from our Heavenly Father and from His Word.

During that period of time, I worked almost an hour away from home at another far away location. The commute gave me an opportunity to have private heart-to-heart talks with God. I always began by thanking Him for His many blessings, acknowledging Him as Lord and Savior over my life, and thanking Him for traveling mercy (especially since I never before had that kind of daily commute traveling a route with so much truck traffic).

The verse that comes to mind is Psalm 91:1, "He that dwelleth in the secret place of the most High shall abide under the shadow of the Almighty." Regardless of where we travel and how far we have to go, there is a hiding place under even the shadow of the Lord God Almighty. We have access to His awesome strength.

One morning, as I was driving to work and saddened in my spirit, I asked God how much longer before we would see the results of our prayers and an improvement in Mom's condition. I expressed to God that it had been three months and Mom just laid there, spending most of her time asleep.

I tried to talk to God rationally, but could not contain my tears and, although I was still driving, I began to cry uncontrollably. A soft still voice simply whispered, "It's time to let her go."

I will remember those words for the rest of my life because they put things into a different perspective and, truthfully, I knew God was right. Her physical body could no longer sustain her, and it would have been selfish for us to expect her to continue to exist in that condition.

It's not that God wasn't hearing our prayers; it was time for Mom to leave this life and that was God's way of preparing me for that day. When God speaks, it's truly time to listen and understand His divine purpose for that particular situation. His Word will come to you when you're in a position to receive and, subsequently, accept it.

The Holy Spirit brought back to my remembrance something my former pastor, Reverend Mother Derris Cargile, had requested. She said that when it was time for her to go, don't pray for her to stay. God hears and answers our prayers and we should be careful what we pray. This woman of God whom I met back in the early 70's was ahead of her time.

As young people, some of the things she said we didn't fully understand but had enough respect for her to consider what we were told. God's servants have always been peculiar people with unusual wisdom. In the end, it's better to be obedient rather than suffer the sacrifice that can occur from disobedience.

Once I had digested God's Words, I was able to pull myself together and told God, "Whatever your decision is, Lord I will honor it."

Thereafter, for the balance of my commute I composed myself and by the time I got to work no one could detect the emotional ordeal I had just experienced. I've found down through the years that a solid relationship with God will sustain you when no one is present to put their arms around you and to console you; remember, God is omnipresent.

That day, after work, I went to visit Mom, arrived before my sister did, and told her that I would make sure I kept in touch with and looked after my sister. My sister wasn't married and had no children. My maternal grandmother had raised me, and my sister had lived with Mom.

I believe Mom was concerned that my sister would be alone when she passed. Mom opened her eyes and looked at me but never spoke a word. It was like the message was received and her expression showed that her heart and mind were both at ease.

At my home, we had been renovating the third floor and removed a wall to make one big room for the children. Anyone who has ever done any kind of home renovation knows, even the smallest project can disorganize the entire household. Summer break was almost over and the first day of school was about to start. The kids were scheduled to return on Tuesday, which was the day after Labor Day, and my classes at a local university started on Wednesday.

Time was of the essence and we were diligently working to get things back in place as much as possible so the first day of school would not be chaotic. The only way to get everything organized within that time frame was to work straight through the weekend, which meant I most likely would not make it to the hospital.

With that particular day being the first Sunday in September, I figured Moms' church members who could not visit during the week would like to visit, and the deacons could possibly see if Mom was up to taking a little communion.

My husband asked several times as the day drew to a close, if I wanted to get cleaned up and run to the hospital. I told him that I wasn't led to go. Over the past three months, we'd prayed a lot of prayers, read numerous Scriptures, and sang a lot of songs. God was going to do what He felt was best. I had made peace with the situation that day I was driving to work on the highway.

When you've been in the midst of a storm and God sends understanding, then you can find peace in the words He has spoken to you. Paul wrote to the Philippians, "And the peace of God, which passeth all understanding, shall keep your hearts and minds through Christ Jesus" (4:7). In this, I drew strength and figured I could spend a little extra time with her on Monday since it would be Labor Day. The kids and their father could grill dinner and we all could eat together when I came home.

My sister went to the hospital on Sunday and some of the church members did come to visit. One thing my sister noticed was that Mom kept looking at her and wherever she moved, Mom's eyes would follow. She said it was strange because most times the medication kept her sleepy, but that day she was very alert. It was an unusual occurrence like the day we were there and out of the clear blue Mom said, "I think I'll go into the kitchen and make myself a sandwich."

Now mind you, she had spoken very few words during the entire time she was hospitalized and never a complete sentence.

Then she said, "I'm going out, will I need my coat?"

It was as though they were the last clear thoughts she had before she collapsed and laid on the floor overnight. Summer had not fully come at that time, so she would have needed a light coat.

Nevertheless, around 2:00 AM on Labor Day, Mom went to sleep in the Lord. Upon entering her room, she looked so peaceful. It was the first time in months I was able to hold her hand and not see her wrench from the pain.

Afterward, an autopsy was performed to see if there was a hidden abnormality that could not be detected while she was alive. The doctors were hoping to determine the underlining cause of the fever and utilize that knowledge to help other patients who may be diagnosed with similar symptoms. Ironically, no indication could be found, and her official cause of death remained FUO, a total mystery.

The clear audible voice of God brought me peace and fortified my faith in Him to know He was making the right decision and all I had to do was accept it. He that hath an ear let him hear God when He speaks (Matt 11:15).

11. The Faith of a Child

The faith of a child resulted in the gift of a $100 pair of sneakers. It was around the Christmas holidays and my husband and I were discussing what we were going to give the children as gifts. My oldest daughter who was approximately 14 years old wanted a special pair of sneakers that cost $100.

At that time, spending $100 for a pair of sneakers for some people wasn't a big deal, but we had three other children for whom we desired to purchase gifts as well. I needed to be practical so that everyone would have a merry Christmas.

Knowing historically how that time of the year was tight for us, I always endeavored to not overspend or be in debt upon entering the New Year. At one time, I was able to put items on lay-a-way and once the holidays arrived, we could have a nice Christmas and not worry about outstanding bills rolling over into the month of January. Yes, K-Mart lay-a-way at lunchtime was my friend.

One evening in prayer, she asked God for the sneakers. I'm talking about the faith of a child. Our children have always gone to church and had personally experienced seeing times where God answered my prayers just because I asked in faith, and then they would partake of the crazy praise that always followed an answered prayer.

ROBIN M. HAILEY

The following Sunday, we went to church and after praise and worship, before bringing his message, Pastor Jason said that God told him that someone asked for a special pair of sneakers for Christmas. He then said, "I know you're here so we're going to wait a few moments and give you an opportunity to come forth."

I've experienced the move of God in different ways and one day, I was in a service with Pastor W.V. Grant and he said, "Robin, God told me to tell you to put $500 in the offering."

There were a lot of people in the service and with Robin being a common name I just knew he wasn't talking to me, but then Pastor Grant stood on top of a chair and said, "Robin Marie, God said put $500 in the basket. He has a special blessing for you."

At that point I knew he was talking to me, I looked at my Mom and she looked at me and I said, "I guess that's me."

Mom could not believe the amount but sat patiently to see what I would do.

At that time, I was once again in need of an extraordinary blessing and was obedient. Now understand, there was no way in the world I would tell my husband what I had done. There would have been turmoil in my home for weeks.

Within a few days surprise checks showed up in the mail and I was able to get our expenses back on track. I was so glad to have obeyed. It was a stretch of faith to give when we personally had such as need.

Back to the sneakers, Pastor Jason continued to minister to the congregation and made another appeal for the person to come forth. At this time, I noticed that my daughter had an unusual look on her face. I told her, "If that is you, get up and go to the front."

Pastor Jason made it clear that you have to move while God is speaking and while the anointing is moving. Do not come to him at the end of the service; it will be too late.

What people fail to realize is that it may not always be for you to experience what He is going to do, but others need to see the move of God and it will encourage them to continue to have faith in Him. When told by God to move, don't hesitate because it may cause you to miss a blessing.

My daughter stepped out into the isle and walked down to the front, at this point tears just rolled down her cheeks, she could not believe what was happening. It was a witness to her and the rest of the congregation that God hears our prayers and it doesn't matter if you are a child or an adult, He waits to hear from us. Our voice has a sound that only relates to us, God does not get it confused with another. When you pray in the secret place of the most high (Psa 91:1), God is sure to reward you openly.

Pastor Jason asked if she was the one who prayed the prayer and she said, "Yes."

The congregation began to get emotional and worship God.

He then asked her what kind of sneakers she asked for and she told him the brand.

Because I always shopped economically, I had no idea what name brand they were talking about.

Then he turned to the choir and asked how much these sneakers cost, and someone said, "Approximately $100."

You could have blown me over with a feather. I said to myself, No wonder she asked God and not me; she knew we didn't have money like that to spend on footwear.

At that point, Pastor Jason took $100 out of his pocket and handed it to my daughter.

I was in awe because out of the hundreds of people who were in that service, God would choose a time such as that to be a blessing to us. I believe the faith that little girl had to pray and humbly ask God for something personal, blessed others and encouraged them to do the same for whatever they stood in need of or had a desire for.

After we purchased the sneakers, I told my daughter to thank God each time she wore them. They were to be a reminder that God does answer prayers and He is no respecter of persons

(Acts 10:34). His blessings and favor flow regardless of race, creed, color, nationality, gender, or age.

12. One Thousand Dollar Challenge

Once we had our last service under the leadership of my former pastor who made plans to relocate to South Carolina, I started looking for another ministry. We were taught well, and I wanted the Holy Spirit to lead me to a ministry that would benefit the family. I had been attending a local multicultural ministry. The people were not ashamed to give God praise and thanks for what He did in their lives. So many people went to that church, that they had two Sunday morning services, and then children's church simultaneously in another part of the building.

The pastor shared an idea with the congregation that God had given to him. It would be an avenue to bless His people and help them get out of debt. According to Malachi 3:10, our tithes are our obligation. Blessings come from the offerings; the offerings are what keep the money flowing. Luke wrote, "For if you give, you will get! Your gift will return to you in full and overflowing measure, pressed down, shaken together to make room for more, and running over. Whatever measure you use to give—large or small—will be used to measure what is given back to you" (Luke 6:38, TLB).

As pastor explained the process and established a time period, God was speaking to my heart to be a part of that opportunity because it would be a blessing to my household and me. In looking at my circumstances, I was trying to figure out how I could put $1,000 in the offering when I had bills that I was currently unable to meet.

The Lord continued to persuade me to write a check and put it in the envelope. I wanted to be obedient for I knew to obey was better than sacrifice (1 Sam 15:22b), but the numbers associated with what I owed kept looming over my head.

The word had come forth on a Sunday and knowing that the next business day was payday, I felt I had nothing to lose so I wrote the check and placed it in the envelope. Real faith is exhibited when you put the check in the envelope to cover the challenge, but don't know when any additional funds will deposit into your account to cover bills. Regardless, whether the next day was payday or not, I was still financially in bad shape.

I had originally planned to send the $1,000 to the mortgage company, but it would not have helped my situation because I was three months behind and facing foreclosure. Mortgage companies in many cases won't accept anything less than what you owe to clear the arrears.

Now I remind you, again I made a decision like this without telling my husband. I learned after several other challenges that God was keeping me covered under the blood of Jesus as I obeyed the Father's requests.

I believe married couples should always share with one another, but if one believes and the other doesn't, sometimes the believing spouse must make a judgment call and trust God. Faith without works is dead (Jam 2:18, 20, 26), so I was obligated to put my faith in God that a miracle would come out of that act of obedience and for making the commitment by trusting Him on that level.

Not many days later, after planting my seed of faith, I received several unexpected checks in the mail. I was able to pay all the bills, get the mortgage back on track, and purchase groceries. All this was after I gave God His 10% off the gross. *What a mighty God we serve!* God proved to me that He had my back; this was yet another time the agreement had to be only between God and me; doubting Thomas could not be included in the mix.

After such a miraculous exhibition of the power of God in my finances, I had a desire to excel in my giving so much so, that my tithes would match my desired gross income. God never intended for His people to be servant to the lender (Prov 22:7). His desire is that we be in health and prosper even as our souls prosper (3 John 1:2). Verse order is important. People tend to seek materialism before spiritualism. Lay up your treasures in heaven (Matt 6:19–21) and by seeking God first, all things that you have need of will be added unto you (Matt 6:33).

You may wonder why I've included so many Scriptures in this writing. The purpose is to show that utilizing God's Word moves His heart. God connects with His Word because it came from Him and when we use His Word, it shows we trust in Him.

The Word of God stands firm and covers so much territory; unless you take time to study it you won't realize how much you are missing. God's Word is an instructional road map for every situation. Second Timothy (2:15) encourages us to, "Study to shew thyself approved unto God, a workman that needeth not to be ashamed, rightly dividing the word of truth." Knowing the Word for yourself personally benefits you and enriches your life because you'll gain a greater understanding of God's purpose for you.

Satan's plan is to prevent the Word of God from being circulated globally; our obligation is to support the spreading of the Word. We can witness to people and as led by the Holy Spirit, sow into areas that facilitate the honest spreading of the gospel. I say it this way because there are people who claim to spread the Word, but their motive is personal gain or to profit by that which should be applied towards kingdom building.

Galatians 6:7 states, "Be not deceived; God is not mocked: for whatsoever a man soweth, that shall he also reap." Let us have a mindset to sow good so that we can reap good." Amos (9:13) tells us that the sower will overtake the reaper. Do you want to be a part of this awesome event? Can you even imagine how it would feel to

ROBIN M. HAILEY

plant a monetary seed into God's kingdom and receive an immediate return?

Reaping is not limited to monetary reaping, but we can reap good when we sow the Word of God into the lives of other people. That's mind blowing, but indicative of how God wants to work in our lives.

Our minds, our health, and our finances are some of the biggest areas of attack by the enemy. If you are worried about not having enough to cover necessities, doubt will take root like the Johnson weed and soon chokes any part of the Word of God and faith in the Word you have managed to hold onto. The Johnson weed grows uncontrollably and destroys everything in its path. It's a very hardy form of a weed and difficult to get rid of. In certain areas it helps stop soil erosion but for farmers it can be a major nightmare.

A worrisome thought that is allowed to remain for too long will begin to affect your health. In some cases, people have worried so much they've developed physical ailments. Heart attacks and strokes can be induced by worry, not just by unhealthy eating habits. Worry causes an imbalance in the body which medical science cannot understand, but Jesus said in John (14:1), "Let not your heart be troubled: ye believe in God, believe also in me." These words of comfort are applicable to the physical, psychological and spiritual state of man's wellbeing. Just a little food for thought: exercise unwavering faith and keep worry at bay.

13. Delayed Doesn't Mean Denied

We can be a partaker of the blessing of Abram through the blood that Jesus shed on Calvary. In Genesis (12:1-3), God instructed Abram to leave his father's house out of the country of his family. God further stated, "And I will bless them that bless thee, and curse him that curseth thee: and in thee shall all families of the earth be blessed" (v3). When God made this proclamation, he didn't specify any particular ethnic group; he said, "all families of the earth be blessed."

Then Paul wrote in Romans (15:4), "For whatsoever things were written aforetime were written for our learning, that we through patience and comfort of the Scriptures might have hope." God's covenant with Abram, if we are in Christ, covers us as well.

Numerous people live paycheck to paycheck but understand one thing, this was never God's principle that His people experience a chronic economic deficiency. Deuteronomy (8:18) says, "But thou shalt remember the LORD thy God: for it is he that giveth thee power to get wealth, that he may establish his covenant which he sware unto thy fathers, as it is this day."

And to reiterate this promise we read the words of Solomon in Proverbs (10:22), "The blessing of the LORD, it maketh rich, and he addeth no sorrow with it." If we obtain our wealth in the proper manner, our blessing will not become a sorrow or a burden to us.

ROBIN M. HAILEY

Many years ago, I worked in the same building with a man who won a Five Million Dollar lottery. He spent money haphazardly, trying to take care of both his ex-wife and girlfriend. When you obtain money like that and showboat, relatives and all kinds of organizations come out of the woodworks. Needless to say, in a few short years he was broke and unemployed. If he had invested the money wisely, or put it in a trust fund and allotted himself a specific amount each month and lived within the perimeters of his allocation, he would have benefited from the residual income.

Residual income is income that you make after your work is done. For instance, I use to be part of Amway. "Amway Business Owners (ABOs) make money when their customers buy Amway products and by building a business where others in your organization sell products" (Google.com). What you earn is based on the volume of products sold by your team members; it is income you do not personally work for.

When God sees fit to send a blessing, we must ask the Holy Spirit to show us how to be good stewards over the blessing. Who knows, you may have a family member leave you big money or as an entrepreneur land a major contract that results in windfall payments. Ask God to show you how to manage the blessing because in most cases, once the money is gone it is gone and everyone who hung around when you had money will be gone as well.

If we do our part, God is sure to do His. If you allow Him, God will show you the people who mean you no good, regardless of the relationship you've maintained with them. if God says, "come out from among them" (2 Cor 6:17), do it quickly so that you will not be swindled out of your blessing.

It's also important to associate with people who are faith walkers. People who will pray for and with you, they will inspire you to do the right thing and encourage you in your walk to make sound decisions. Beware of people with hidden agendas. Are they in it for what they can get, or are they genuine supporters?

I've made these statements because when people feel you have nothing to offer, they can't be bothered with you, but when they see the evidence that the hand of God is upon your life and prosperity follows you, their attitude toward you changes.

If you've made up your mind to believe God for a certain thing and you share your belief with someone who claims to support you but later, they shoot down what you believe, you may discover that their negativity stemmed from jealousy. True faith walkers tread on thin ice, whereas, others may be comfortable standing on the brink just watching. Be encouraged to walk by faith and not by sight (2 Cor 5:7), understand that everyone isn't built to walk this walk.

The adversary knows when we are the apple of God's eye (Psa 17:8; Zec 2:8) and his position is to prevent us from obtaining the best God has to offer. God is allowing us access through the orifice of His eye, not everyone qualifies to be in this position because some people refuse to be submissive. It's not a place you can bribe your way into our pull rank on someone to gain access. You may have to fight a little harder to reach the mark, you may have to sacrifice more, you may have to cry alone at times, but don't become weary in well doing (Gal 6:9), the reward in the end is greater than the struggle.

There is a misconception that Christians cannot be or should be wealthy. If God blesses us to have wealth, live in a nice home, and wear nice clothes, as compensation for blessing Him and the House of Prayer and His servants, what's wrong with it? Nothing! Genesis (13:3) tells us that Abram was very rich in cattle, in silver, and in gold. In his richness he was righteous.

If we remain humble and acknowledge God as our source, we can have what we say, if we believe when we pray. In Mark (11:24) Jesus said, "Therefore I say unto you, What things soever ye desire, when ye pray, believe that ye receive them, and ye shall have them."

Proverbs (18:21) reminds us that death and life are in the power of the tongue. Speak life and prosperity into your finances but remember to remain humble when the increase arrives.

ROBIN M. HAILEY

As children we use to say, "Sticks and stones can break your bones, but words will never hurt you." This statement is so far from the truth. People have been known to take their own lives as a result of the words others have spoken to them, about them or over them. Our words carry weight, and in some cases it's better not to say anything rather than speak words that will turn against us or someone else in the end.

If you have faith to believe God will bless you, just speak by faith into the atmosphere. Decree and declare without wavering and it shall be, but if you are a doubter and consistently speak doubt into the atmosphere it will cancel the words you previously spoke in faith. Don't release the spirit of confusion into your personal space. Remember, "a double minded man is unstable in all his ways," (Jam 1:8) so make sure there is continuity in the words you speak and that they remain positive.

I said all of what's written above to make this point: Delay does not mean denied. I became so passionate with this notion of speaking to my income that it would substantially increase, while I was employed, I began giving tithes on what I wanted my gross income to be; I call this, "tithing up." Remember, God loves a cheerful giver (2 Cor 9:7). Here is where one would say to oneself, "If my finances are challenged and I end up with more month than money, how in heavens name could I consider tithing towards where I want my gross income to be?"

Logically speaking, this may make the least amount of sense out of anything that I've said up to this point but here is what I did. I took an analytical look at the budget and went to God with the tangible numbers, for some reason if I paid bills, I didn't have an adequate amount left to buy groceries and if I purchased groceries, I ran short on the bills. After working the figures, I told God I actually needed another thousand dollars in the budget in order to meet monthly expenses.

Another circumstance that was constant, involved a two-family home that I owned. Many times, the tenant would run late with the rent or other unexpected things would occur leaving me even shorter when I needed the money. Funds that should have come in to help the budget were being delayed and regardless whether the tenant paid their rent or not, I was still responsible for making sure the mortgage was paid.

I had really been working toward a promotion for several years while I saw people all around me get upgraded. I witnessed an intern with a major outside of our line of business, get mentored, and subsequently promoted to the level that I was trying to obtain; and for some unknown reason, I kept getting passed over. I guess it didn't help when I questioned management about how it was that certain individuals were a recipient of the kind of instruction I had been requesting.

Management's explanation was that I didn't have the aptitude to do the work. Then they would further say, "You need a four-year degree and right now you only have a two-year degree."

In essence, taking a shrewd approach they worded comments whereas they would not get hit with discrimination charges, but I knew where they were coming from. Other people have mentioned being in similar situations, it doesn't matter where you work; politics can be found everywhere. I tried not to become angry or bitter about what I dealt with on a regular basis, but it did cause me to experience sleepless nights.

I didn't understand how people could feel so comfortable in asking me questions that related to different functionality aspects of the business but didn't want to compensate me for the knowledge I had acquired down through the years. My perception was, this is usury. In dealing with this I resorted to kindly responding, "I don't quite remember how to do that."

Now you and I both know this didn't go over well, but they couldn't make me provide an answer, nor could they further penalize or harass me for not providing an answer. Sometimes it's not what you say but how you say it, so avoiding a sarcastic tone I was able to get away with it unpunished. Under the circumstances, what did I have to lose? Apparent damage was already done.

Not long thereafter, we had a system change. When people realized that they needed to know tasks that they always had considered to be beneath them, things in the office became very interesting. I said to myself, *God, you have a funny sense of humor. I love it.*

In the end, the entire process humbled a lot of people and I was encouraged to be more cooperative because I knew the process and whether I received recognition for knowing it or not, it didn't change what I knew.

Nevertheless, an offer was made for me to take a lateral position in a different department. I had previously told myself I would never accept a lateral move because that's not what I wanted. I was looking to be promoted. Still being a member of a prophetic ministry, God gave me a Word through my pastor. God said that I would change positions. I was happy about the change but also accepted the reality that it would not be a promotion. Not many weeks later I was offered a lateral move and, in faith, accepted it. The hiring manager was aware of my situation and had firsthand knowledge of the quality of my work. I was told that sometimes in the corporate world, people are labeled, and the only practical option is to get away from decision makers who are holding you back. After I made the move, approximately 90 days later, I was promoted to the level I had long awaited.

When you're faced with a situation such as this, try to the best of your ability not to break the stride in your walk with the Lord. Continuity carries a lot of weight and it shows God how serious you are about your relationship with him. The adversary is notorious for painting a picture of doom and gloom, but God said, "My grace is sufficient" (2 Cor 12:9), and with this kind of strength supporting us, we can move on to bigger and better things.

Greater victories sometimes require a greater sacrifice, and when you see God working in the mist of you, let there be spontaneity in your response to Him. Don't procrastinate and think *this is not the right place* or *I'll wait until I get to church.* Life in general and other responsibilities will cause you to forget to give God what is due unto Him. You never want to treat God with an attitude of ingratitude.

I've been in Walgreen's and asked the cashier if I had any rewards available. When I found out the rewards brought my balance down to less than $5.00, I verbally said, "Praise the Lord and shout Hallelujah." A few people laughed, but I explained that the savings left me money for something else.

The delayed promotion was a set up; for not even six months later God spoke again through the prophet and said, "Now I'm pulling you off the job."

I was floored, not realizing at that time that God had a better plan for me, and it would give me the extra monthly income I had humbly requested.

14. Downsized for a Blessing

My new position put me in a better place financially, the struggle wasn't as demanding, and I could somewhat make ends meet. When you are mindful that you are spending God's money, you have a tendency to make wiser decisions regarding what to pay in full and what to make partial payments on until the next statement is sent.

As it so happened, I was working for a research and development company that wasn't doing well and they were looking to downsize. Early retirement packages were being offered. As a result of my years of service I qualified for a package. After I looked at the numbers and did the math, basically God was giving me the extra I had requested but, on the flipside, it would leave me unemployed. It has been often said, be careful what you ask for, but also know that God always has our best interest in mind. Regardless of what may come, our destiny remains in His hands.

For a few weeks I pondered over the decision whether to stay or leave. God's instructions were to, "Take the package."

Here I am, being pulled out of my comfort zone. I was meeting my monthly budget, but there was nothing extra. We should always have a goal one way or another to save some money. The economy can be shaky, and 401k's can be compromised.

Many other employees opted to not take the package. I guess they figured that based upon those who left, their jobs would be safe. When such decisions are made, it's not contingent upon numbers alone, decision makers look at talent and where it counts the most. If positions are deemed to add to operating expenses and overhead, those positions are the first to be cut.

After the departure of some of the employees who were close to retirement, the company still needed to further cut the staff. On various mornings, managers with the accompaniment of security, would show up at the desk of targeted employees, allow them to gather personal belongings, take their badges, and walk them to the door. Although that procedure appeared to be heartless, it became necessary because when other employees found out they were being involuntarily terminated, they sabotaged the projects they were working on. Henceforth, no one could easily pick up where they left off.

The executive managers tried to keep those procedures under wraps but when you work with a tight knit group the word spreads. I was grateful to God that He gave me guidance to take the package and not be subjected to the humiliation of being terminated in that manner. I was being downsized so God could use those conditions to bless me. I wasn't sure what would come next after my departure and knowing I would not have a job, out of obedience, I stepped out on faith.

It's important to know when God is speaking and decipher His voice from the voice of the enemy. In the end, after being unemployed for about nine months, I was blessed to get hired by a national real estate company paying $17,000 a year more than the position I had with the research and development company. During my period of unemployment, the bills got paid, we had food on the table, and based upon whatever came in during that time, I still brought my tithes to the storehouse.

Ironically, with the new firm, I applied for one position but after the interview it was determined that I qualified for a higher position that also had a vacancy. I choose the one that paid more.

Of course, the position that paid more came with more responsibility, but it gave me exposure to VP's across the country.

After working in the new company for four years, my base salary increased by $13,000. There is no way you can tell me that God doesn't fortify His numbers with His glory. My income without my spouse's was now six figures, and I remained faithful with my tithes, especially in knowing how much God had my back.

Take the limits off, and experience firsthand what God can do. He has given us resources within ourselves to make things happen. Each of us has received a measure of faith (Rom 12:3). Everything depends on what you decide to do with yours.

15. Just Do It

While working for the real estate company, I supervised a staff of six. One of my direct reports was pregnant, and on a particular day she complained that her lower back was hurting. She wasn't close enough to her due date to be concerned that the baby was on his way. Her doctor said that she may have slept in the wrong position and the discomfort she was feeling was the end result.

My crew had worked with me long enough to understand the relationship I had with the Lord. Whereas, I was concerned that in the workplace it would be an issue, I found to the contrary, that my faith encouraged them. There were times when, because of corporate growth, things would escalate to borderline chaotic. With every acquisition there came more sites to equip and more customers to service. There were a few situations where personality conflicts would occur, and I found myself going into the office early, just to lay hands on the cubical panels throughout my staff's work area so we could have a peaceful and productive day.

As we worked through the afternoon, I could tell that employee wasn't feeling any better, but she didn't want to go home. I had an office with a door, so I closed the door and quietly went before the Lord asking what I could do. When it's been confirmed that there's a call on your life, you have to gain confidence in knowing that when you ask God a question you can expect to get an answer. I remember going before the Lord asking on behalf of my cousin's wife what I could do. God provided an answer that resulted in victory over the situation.

I always kept a small bottle of oil in my desk, so after my conversation with the Lord, I sent my employee an instant message asking her to come into my office. At first, she thought she was in trouble because I never indicated why I wanted to see her and didn't ask her to bring a document that may possibly have had an issue. When she came in, I told her I was led of the Lord to anoint her lower back with a little oil, in the name of Jesus, and asked if she would mind if I did so. Now, you know God had to be in that plan because in the workplace there are some things you just shouldn't do, but that action was of necessity.

She gave me permission and I did it quickly as instructed by the Lord and sent her back to her desk.

At the end of the workday, I asked how she felt, and she said that she felt worse.

Those words hit me hard, and my heart dropped.

She slowly left and got into her car. I did likewise and as I drove home, I sought the Lord, "What went wrong? God, I did as you instructed and prayed with faith that the pain would leave, and healing would be manifested."

When I arrived home, I sat in the driveway and before I went into the house, I asked God if there were something else I should have done, but there was silence from heaven.

The next day I went into the office as usual, said a prayer before my staff arrived, and after they did, I told the lead person that when the expecting Mom arrived, I wanted to see her immediately.

When the Mommy-to-be came in, she basically bounced into my office, which took me by surprise. I had to do a double take. I asked how she felt, and she said that she felt fine.

The day prior, upon leaving the office, she felt worse, but by the time she got home the pain was completely gone.

That lifted such a weight off my spirit man I cannot verbalize how I felt. At that point, I remembered God's Words from the day before, "Just do it."

Others may have experienced similar situations when you know you heard the voice of the Lord, by faith did as instructed but the result wasn't what you expected. There are times the test is not necessarily for the person you've been led to pray for, but it's for you. Can you trust God when you don't get an expected answer? Can you trust God when you don't receive an immediate answer? Can you rest, assured that the God you serve will never mislead you? I've posed three questions back-to-back, just to get you thinking.

As the months went on, that employee continued to come to work and for the life of us because she was so big, we couldn't figure out how she even got behind the wheel of the car. Every day she came in we would sigh, but she assured us she was fine. Her doctor said she was fit to continue to work and her husband wasn't protesting, so there she was.

The ladies had discussions about childbirth, and she mentioned that a midwife delivered her first child and they had planned to use a midwife to also deliver this baby. Not long afterward, the time came when she was no longer permitted to drive but she was okay with it because she was so close to her due date. She wasn't home many days before she went into labor. My lead person advised me she got a call early that morning from the pregnant employee and, yes, she was in full labor.

As we got closer to lunchtime the update was that our co-worker was still in labor and they weren't sure how much longer before the baby would come. We were then at 3:00 PM and she was still in active labor.

I told my team leader, "The next time you speak to the Mommy-to-be, if they suggest she needs a cesarean, don't fight it, just do it."

When the next call was received, my lead employee relayed the message and during that time I was in prayer again seeking the face of God to reassure myself that I heard the Lord accurately.

Later she told me her husband said, "I thought we decided we would go with the midwife."

She had replied to him, "but if Robin said to go with the cesarean, there must be a reason and we'll do it."

When you find that people have that kind of confidence in you it can be scary. Her labor progressed but they noticed the baby appeared to be in distress and it was suggested she have a cesarean. Her reply was, "Let's do it."

Later that afternoon once all was said and done and things settled down, she called to say thank you. Come to find out, the umbilical cord was wrapped around the baby's neck and if she had continued with a regular delivery the baby would not have made it.

It's one thing to say you have faith that God speaks to you and you personally do as instructed, but it takes another level of faith to do as God has spoken as it relates to others. I had a certain amount of apprehension in speaking this word because I felt I was imposing into a matter that was personal to another. It is important to maintain a strong relationship with God so His voice and instructions will be unmistakable when you hear it.

My coworker gave birth to a very healthy baby boy who has grown up to be a fine young man. If I had not done what thus saith the Lord and found out later that my doubt resulted in the baby being stillborn, I don't think I could have lived with myself. In the end, sometimes we have to, "just do it."

16. Purge and Pack

We stayed in the HUD house for approximately 23 years, went through a number of tenants until the final one moved in, and she resided with us for more than five years. It was stated in the tenant/landlord agreement that we were renting to a single, nonsmoking female, with a dog. I'm not that fond of dogs but he was her companion. He stayed inside except when she walked him or took him to the vet. She kept him clean and he was so quiet that we hardly ever heard him bark.

In the process of interviewing perspective tenants, my insistence on a nonsmoker was firm. My youngest son had asthma and from previous tenants, smoke was an issue. What we discovered was the small openings around the radiator risers would allow smoke to come up from the first floor. To most people this may not have appeared to be a big deal but sometimes the second floor where everyone spent most of their time, would smell like an ashtray.

The situation escalated when smokers entertained guests who were also smokers. We could wave our hands and see the smoke move in the atmosphere; sometimes we had to run the big air conditioner just to vent the smoke out of the air and it wasn't always warm outside. When it came time to rent that last go around, I said, "no smokers," and that was non-negotiable.

People are too funny. One couple said, "We smoke, but will only smoke outside." Now, you and I both know, if it's icy cold in the middle of the winter and almost midnight there is no way in the world, they'll bundle up to go outside for a cigarette. Sorry folks, no can do.

Things were good for a long time with the last tenant until intermittently her brother and sister began staying with her because they could not keep a place of their own. Much to my displeasure they both were smokers and although they were aware of the house rule, no one wanted to abide by it, especially if someone needed a cigarette in the middle of the night or it was very cold outside.

For months, I went to God in prayer about the entire situation. I told God, "I am tired of being a landlord, tired of the cigarette smoke, tired of living in a home that's not finished; just TIRED. Lord, I want a single-family home."

Initially, our goal as stated previously, was to buy the two-family dwelling, stay for a while, save enough money to purchase a single-family home, and rent out our floor. With all the financial challenges we experienced, that never happened, but *my desire* was still in my heart.

One Sunday while in service, Apostle Carr, who was my Pastor at that time said, "There are three people who asked God to move," and she looked at me and said, "You are one of them."

I smiled because it was true. For me it was a confirmation once again that God does hear our prayers and when we're in a right relationship with Him, He will gladly answer.

A subsequent word followed, instructing me to start looking for the new house. I did so immediately. There were days I would sit in my car and pray, asking God to show me where I was to look. If you go out blindly you could be looking forever and in the wrong direction. It was now almost two years later, and I was still looking: looking in the newspaper; searching on the Internet; and just driving through certain neighborhoods as led by the Holy Spirit.

It seems that something should have materialized from all that searching, but I've learned that God will give you instructions just to see if you will follow them.

In the meantime, God instructed me to start packing, I began to bring boxes home. This is where the opposition began. No one in my home understood what was going on. I told them, "Now is the time to purge and pack. We've been here for 23 years and it's time to let some of this junk go. I've got news for you folks; all this stuff isn't going to the new house."

I diligently tried to keep the house the way I wanted the new one to look, but you can't put new wine in an old bottle (Matt 9:17; Mark 2:22). I was fighting a losing battle. At that point, I dealt with opposition on a whole new level. It was frustrating. No one saw the vision the way I did.

At one point, I thought about throwing in the towel, evicting the tenant, and opening up the whole house, but that didn't resolve the fact that the HUD house had rooms that were still incomplete. My husband was one who had great ideas but didn't finish anything he started; one project was badly needed so I agreed to let him do it but only because I was tired of being embarrassed when people came in the back door.

We primarily entered through the kitchen because our cars were parked in the back of the house. Frequent visitors would do the same because it was easier. To walk into the kitchen meant you could look straight through the house right into the bathroom and the tub surround was badly worn. I must say he accomplished most of the reinstallation of the wallboards without tying up the bathroom for too long, but the job was never one hundred percent completed.

As I continued to get rid of items that I knew I didn't want to take to the new house, I was trying to encourage others to do the same. God's next instruction was to start putting boxes on the porch to show the devil that, "Yes, we are going to move."

The irony behind this was that we had no money to even consider a down payment. I vividly remembered how God orchestrated the first move and had faith in Him that if He was giving specific directions, He had a plan for this move as well.

You cannot allow fear or pessimism to enter. Your faith must be strong to believe God's instructions. Remember, faith without works is dead (Jam 2:18, 20, 26). I've seen people get a Word but decline to act upon it because their finances were not lining up with the prophecy. Faith is believing when you cannot see the outcome and you have no way to make things come to pass. If you can see it, then it's not faith. If you can make it happen, then you don't need God.

We obtained a dumpster and got rid of a lot of stuff. If an item had not been touched in more than a year or two, it was a candidate to be tossed.

17. Love at First Sight

On a particular Monday, I was looking through the Sunday newspaper and saw a listing for a home in the neighboring town. Because we had spent most of Sunday in church, I had missed the official open house. With the address in hand, I took a ride and when I pulled up in front of the house my eyes were wide opened. It was love at first sight.

It was a beautiful house. It looked just like me and it was in the town I actually preferred to move to, but felt it was out of my reach financially. My two youngest children had just started classes at the community college and, at that time, neither of them was driving. Moving too far would create a transportation issue for all of us. The location was absolutely perfect where I could maintain my obligations at the church and not have an extensive daily commute to work.

I decided to take a closer look at the house and had the nerve to pull into the driveway not realizing someone was home and watching me. I got out and walked the property. The yard was a nice size, fenced in with a gym set and gazebo. This house was no comparison to the house I wanted to move out of; the only thing they had in common was the lot size. From the sign on the front lawn, I jotted down the name and phone number of the realtor. We played telephone tag for days without actually speaking to each other.

One afternoon, before my husband went to work, I encouraged him to take a ride with me and look at the house. By then he was discouraged because so much time had gone by and to him, I was trying to do something that was financially impossible. Remember, I've previously said, "With God, nothing shall be impossible" (Luke 1:37).

We pulled up in front of the house and the seller was standing in the driveway. I told him I had stopped by a few times to look at the house and even parked in the driveway. He said, "I know. My wife told me someone came by and appeared to be very interested."

I informed him that I had reached out to the realtor several times, but we kept missing each other. He told me that the realtor was actually his daughter and he would give her a call. At that time, she was managing two careers simultaneously and sometimes things got a little hectic for her.

Not many days hence, we hooked up with the realtor and arranged to see the interior of the house. It was jaw-droppingly beautiful. The interior had 3,200 square feet of living space: five bedrooms, one of which was a master suite; two and a half bathrooms; a walk-in cedar closet which led to a separate area that could be used as a prayer room; a finished basement; and a two-car garage.

The prospect of having a prayer room was monumental to me because in my effort to pack and place some items on the porch, one of them was a wooden chair I had dedicated for prayer and kneeled at it in the dining room. Space had long since been an issue and at times it wasn't safe to lie on the living room floor in front of the wall unit. Early in the mornings, I would be there and if someone came down from the third floor I would have to say, "Don't step on me."

Needless to say, it wasn't funny to hear a voice out of the blue in a dark room. I just knew one morning I would get stomped or something stupid would happen.

One day, I came home from work and saw this rectangular black bag lying in the driveway. After parking my car, I went over and picked it up. All I heard was wooden pieces clanking inside and realized it was my chair. Someone had thrown it into the driveway and completely destroyed it.

At first, I was angry, but after pulling myself together, I said, "You know what devil, God is going to give me a prayer room. The chair served its purpose but breaking it isn't a showstopper."

Even God, who quickeneth the dead calleth those things which be not as though they were (Rom 4:17). I realized it was nothing but the adversary because out of all the stuff that was on the porch, my dedicated chair was the only item that was touched.

> The Lord was doing it one more time
> and each step fortified my faith in the
> Promise Keeper.

18. Time to Reveal the Money Pit

As we commenced our discussions with the realtor, we knew it was time for her to see the home we wanted to sell. This is where part of the miracle comes in. Do you remember I told you that my husband didn't finish any project he started? Well, not one room between the second and third floors was complete. Something in each room was lacking. Truth be told, I had tolerated that situation for as long as I could and being at the end of my rope, I was ready to let the house go without any reservation.

Several years prior, we had a fire in the kitchen that was caused by squirrels that built a nest in the back wall of the porch. All that debris had spontaneously combusted. When I got the call, I left work in a hurry and prayed all the way home, "Lord let me maintain my composure and I pray everyone got out of the house safely."

At that time my two youngest children were home with the sitter, and I didn't yet know if everyone was safe. You know how it is to get a generic call whereas the caller is not trying to send you into a panic; it's a call where you ask no questions, just move.

As the firefighters broke into the wall all this debris started falling out. I thought squirrels had been jumping from the tree branches to run across my roof onto our neighbors' roof. Little did

I realize, they had access to the inside of the wall via a small opening they had created in my siding.

God is so good, and favor is bestowed upon you when you are honest with your tithes. The insurance paid for the repairs to the dwelling itself. They also compensated me for all the canned goods I lost in the pantry. Our local supermarket had just run their annual can-can sale and my pantry was stocked. The microwave also sat in the pantry and the portable dishwasher was positioned in front of the pantry. Although neither appliance appeared to have been damaged, they gave me funds to replace them.

The adjustor also noted the missing cabinet over the stove. I told him it had once contained my grandmother's china and one evening after we had gone to bed, it fell off the wall. God is once again so good. He could not compensate me for the china, but the insurance covered replacing the cabinet and the balance of the parquet flooring.

To stretch the insurance money, we did some of the work ourselves. We basically gutted the entire kitchen and replaced cabinets and the counter. Based upon the previous counter, I measured the space so that I could retain the sink, it was an unusual green porcelain fixture, plus it was deep. When the carpenter came to install the cabinets and counter that we had purchased from a raw wood company, he could not believe I was the one who took the measurements. Everything fit perfectly. I followed God's directions because I knew there was no room for error.

After all that, I still felt it would be a challenge to sell the house, but I had a consistent Word from the Lord. He reconfirmed time and time again, "Yes, you shall move."

One Saturday as I stood in the kitchen looking at the molding and other areas where I figured we could attempt to complete; I told the Lord it would will help the house look a little more presentable.

Ironically, the next day in service God opted to give another Word through the mouth of the Prophet. He instructed me to not do another thing to the house. He said, "You will get more for the selling of the house than it's worth."

I said, "Lord I know this is you; no one else was home when we had this personal conversation."

I could rest assured that a miracle was in store for me because at that time real estate was booming and it was a buyers' market.

If you wait on the Lord, and maintain your faith in Him, you will never be ashamed, regardless of how things may appear (Psa 25:3; Rom 10:11). God understands our predicaments and our concerns and will never set us up to fail.

When you have a relationship with God you can go to Him at any time with any situation. In my spirit I just communed with Him expressing my desires. Previously, we had worked with a realtor from another agency and the amount I was told the house would sell for was an insult.

Now, I know it needed work, but she was just about asking me to give it away. We were not talking about structural repairs. They were all cosmetic. We contracted with her to list the house for 30 days and with no prospective buyers in site we allowed the contract to expire. Basically, her suggestions were not parallel with the prophecy God had spoken.

On the day my new realtor came to the house all I could do was hold my breath waiting for the shoe to fall. From the outside it looked fine but once you got inside it told the real story. She was like, "Oh my." There were no holes in the walls and things as such, but you could tell that projects were incomplete.

Although we had put vinyl siding on the house and upgraded all the windows it didn't compensate for that which was needed inside. The realtor said she had been selling houses for a long time and this one, although it could be a challenge, would sell. She was optimistic and after telling her what we were doing to purge and pack, she gave ideas on how to stage the house for viewing appointments. The key was to emphasize the space and possibilities.

I told her that we would all do well once the deal came to an end; God had made me a promise. The realtor stated she could tell that one of our problems was we had outgrown the house. I replied that we were aware of this and the upcoming move was a good opportunity to purge items that I know we would not take to our new home.

I had always been one who hated clutter, but my husband is one who didn't like to throw anything away unless forced to do so. We represented that old cliché, "Opposites attract." If I didn't put my foot down, we could have been living in hoarder conditions and that was not happening on my watch. Still today, *I hate clutter*.

When your possessions are numerous, you automatically run into two problems:

> (1) you cannot keep the house as tidy as you would like; and

> (2) it gives the devil too many places to hide.

When I go into spiritual warfare, I want to be able to hit every corner. Honestly people, if you have items you have not used in a year or two, it may be time to give them a new home, especially when it comes to appliances that are in excellent working order. You can give to the Goodwill or an organization that helps families who need to start over. Just make sure it's of good quality and clean.

All through my process of looking for a new home, I had advised my tenant we were making plans to sell the house. I don't think she believed it would happen because so much time had passed since I made the initial statement. As we proceeded in compiling the money for the down payment the *For Sale* sign was posted in front of the house.

I continued to pack and believe God to provide the money needed to make the move happen. All we had was the funds in our checking account to cover our monthly recurring expenses, and there was nothing substantial in savings to cover a purchase of this magnitude.

After making an offer on the new house and our offer being accepted, we were on our way to moving into my dream house and the contract prompted the sellers to resume their packing. Later, I learned that another buyer wanted the home but after several attempts they could not get a mortgage. It reminded me so much of what had occurred in the purchase of the house I was now selling. The Lord was doing it one more time and each step fortified my faith in the promise keeper.

19. We Don't Want to Move

During this pre-move process the real opposition began. I found that family members were not as willing as I was to move. In order to show the house to prospective buyers, it needed to be neat and tidy. It appeared that every time I would clean up one area, I would find a mess somewhere else. I would remind the kids to pick up their stuff and make their beds.

On my final walkthrough, I would have to knock myself out to do what they didn't. Most people will agree, after a while, this becomes tiresome and makes you want to throw up your arms and say, "Forget it." My driving force was God's promise and my desire to move.

The next opposition was to deal with a tenant who now refused to be cooperative. She was comfortable where she was, the rent was very affordable, and she was close to public transportation. Overall, she was a very sweet lady. My desire was to give her more than enough notice so she could find a place, vacate the first floor, and give us an opportunity to thoroughly clean the apartment once it was vacant.

At this point, not much progress was being made, it was difficult to be in a place where you are trying to sell and buy a home simultaneously. I would never suggest this approach to anyone

ROBIN M. HAILEY

unless this is your only option. There are too many things that could go wrong and you could be left without a permanent residence for weeks or stuck carrying two mortgages.

The tenant eventually moved, and we called in a crew to help clean up the kitchen and freshen up the walls. Like I said, her brother and sister were smokers, and everything had a smoke film on it. One of the guys suggested we sand blast the ceiling fans, but it was wiser to replace them. I know he was being humorous, but they were very dirty. I don't think they had been cleaned since the last time I had cleaned them, and when I saw the inside of the oven, all I could say was, "Oh Jesus." Heavy Duty Easy Off was my best friend that day.

The next recommendation to push the HUD house to sell was to have an open house. As I've said before, most open houses are held on Sundays. To my understanding, it's always better that the homeowner not be present. The realtor would take care of everything. On Sundays the children and I would be in church and normally didn't come home until late. Most open house sessions would be over by around 3:00 PM so this worked well for us.

The old guy (husband) was my personal challenge. He worked the night shift and swing shifts. He came home Sunday mornings and slept during the day in preparation for his next shift. Fortunately for us, we had a 30' travel trailer sitting in the driveway. I fixed it up, ran electric power so he could use the furnace to stay warm, and he slept out there.

Funny thing about that, although selling the trailer was not part of the deal there were people who wanted to buy it as well. "Hey, let's make it a package deal," some suggested.

The driveway was huge. We parked our cars as well as the trailer on the property and still had plenty of available space. I wasn't willing to sell the trailer, although we could not take it to the new house. The lots were the same size, except the old house was deep and the new house had a wide lot and sat on a corner. We ended up putting the trailer in storage.

20. A Successful Open House

One open house did the trick. A neighbor who lived two houses down from us saw the house as an investment. She had a crew who worked with her to flip houses. She made an offer and we accepted it. The buyer was adamant that the entire house was cleaned out before she would close. I assured her that everything would be removed when she was ready to take her final walkthrough. We bumped heads a number of times through the process. She spoke very broken English and my Spanish is so rusty it squeaks, but we made it work.

On moving day, while in the process of packing the truck, the realtor called in a panic. She said the buyer said that if the basement wasn't cleaned out, we would have no closing. I told the realtor I had assured the buyer the entire house would be immaculate. The realtor went back to the buyer and advised her we would keep our word, but at that point I was hot. I hung up the phone, went out the door and down the street rebuking the devil as I marched. Mind you, it was the end of January, wet and cold outside. I didn't stop to grab my coat. All I knew was that it was time to bring the devil under spiritual arrest.

Have you ever been in a position when enough was enough and you knew it was time to take control? My demeanor and actions scared the movers. All the guys jumped into the back of the truck. My son and his friend were in the basement packing up a few more items when his friend said, "I hear someone screaming."

My son listened and realized it was me. He replied, "That's my Mom. Oh goodness, what happened?"

At that point I was going in. I said, "I've had enough from this lady; she will not leave us alone to do what we said we would do."

I marched down the street praying out loud in my prayer language, taking no prisoners. I walked all the way to her house and back. The Lord would not allow me to go up her stairs and ring the bell. I believe that action would have ruined the deal. By the time I returned to my home, the moving men were peeking out from inside the truck.

Their foreman said, "You know something, I admire what you did. In the Spirit you were taking control over the situation, and I need to do that more often."

As he spoke, I discovered that he attended a local church that my family had visited on a regular basis and I knew he was part of a good ministry. Sometimes people need to see your faith in action. Depending upon the situation, you need to do more than talk. Act upon what you believe, and watch God do the rest.

After the drama was over, the men completed packing the truck and pulled out of the driveway. No sooner than they left, the buyer and her husband showed up at the door, "Is the basement clean?"

I said, "The truck just left."

She asked again, "Is the basement clean?"

I repeated, "The truck just left."

Then in an angry voice, she said, "I'm calling my lawyer."

I said, "Call your lawyer, but like I said, the truck just left, and we will make sure the basement is clean."

I called the realtor and explained that the truck had just left, and because I would not let the buyer see the basement she stormed off and said there would be no closing.

Overall, I saw this as another attempt for the enemy to ruffle my feathers, but I had a promise from God and was standing on faith that we would have a closing and on that day. I would not be stuck with two houses.

The buyer made arrangements with the realtor to see the house the next day and do a final walkthrough. As they went from one room to another, I sat on the steps in the hallway praying in my prayer language. I know they were wondering what was going on because they primarily spoke Spanish. English was their second language. But, what I was speaking was to God and not comprehensible by man.

After they had walked through the entire house and returned to the front door I asked, "So, do we close?"

She said, "Yes."

In a loud voice with much joy I exclaimed, "Gracias, Jesús", that is to say, "Thank You, Jesus," in Spanish.

I wanted her to comprehend what I was saying and understand that my gratitude was to Jesus. All she and her husband could do was smile.

That little lady had been a thorn in my side through the whole process but I also knew she was predestined to be instrumental in purchasing my current home so I could buy the new one. On the 26th of January, we officially closed on both homes and walked away with more than the house was worth just like God has said; it was BIG money.

21. Can't Nobody Sell – Can't Nobody Buy

Before I go into this section, I will say what you read may seem unbelievable, but the events that occurred took my faith to a greater level.

After moving into my new home, things were pretty good. As a result of our not-so-perfect credit, the interest rate on the mortgage was high but the goal was to pay the mortgage at that rate for one year and then refinance at a lower rate.

I still remained faithful in my tithing. I planned for it and looked forward to being able to refinance and, hopefully, thereafter apply extra money toward the principle and pay off the house sooner.

Now is when things take an interesting turn. Six months after moving into the new house, where the taxes were more than the mortgage I had paid on the home that I sold, as a result of the sluggish real estate market, I lost my job!

Three months after that, my mother-in-law's health took a turn for the worse and we had to fly back and forth to California. Sadly, she passed.

Nine months after burying Mom, my husband passed, and through all of this, I was still unemployed with no prospect of employment.

When you've been out of work for too long, it becomes more difficult to convince someone to hire you based upon previous experience. If you're challenged in obtaining full-time employment, opt for part-time and fill in other times with volunteer work. It looks better on your resume.

My husband had passed at home and, although he had a good life insurance policy, the company would not release any funds until they had confirmation from the county medical examiner that he died of natural causes.

Because of the heavy volume, our county coroner's office had a three-month backlog and did not allow any kind of expedite regardless of your situation. I'm sure under court order, in extreme circumstances, they had cases that had to be expedited but under what is considered a normal incident such as mine, I had to wait.

With no money to pay the mortgage, the house went into default. I had retired from the Bell system many years before, but my pension was only enough to cover recurring monthly expenses, buy food, keep the car on the road, etc. There wasn't enough to cover the mortgage.

Of course, you know that after default the house went into foreclosure and was subsequently added to the sheriff's sale. I'm not sure what the average timeframe is for this process, but my timeframe stretched well beyond the norm. I'm once again stressing the importance of being faithful, diligent, and obedient to God. When Jesus referred to His Heavenly Father, he said, "Nothing shall be impossible unto him" (Matt 19:26).

On one particular Sunday, after my pastor, Apostle Maria Carr, brought forth her message, she was led to call a prayer line and God said that He had a Word for everyone who had come to church that day. We were instructed to bring a special offering to give unto the Lord. The offering was not for the pastor.

It was an unusual Sunday because not a lot of people were present that day but later, I learned that God used that as an opportunity to bless those who pressed their way to be in His presence. I gathered what few dollars I had and walked up to the prophet and placed my offering in the basket.

Apostle looked me in my eyes, and she said, "Can't nobody sell. Can't nobody buy."

All I could do was cry. At that time my youngest son and daughter were living at home and they were the only people who knew the house was on the sheriff's list.

Hearing those words was a relief to me. It was confirmation that God had heard my prayers, seen my tears, and felt my pain.

Once everyone had been ministered to, only then did Apostle let us know that God said that it wasn't the amount of our offering that mattered. It was about our obedience. I've been in services where God has expressed a special request of the people; some respond right away, some take their time in responding, and some don't respond at all. On that day, for me it was a blessing to rapidly respond and not be deterred by the fact that all I had to my name was a few dollars.

In the meantime, the roof developed a leak. During a hard rain, water would drip through the drop stairs to the attic. Apostle said she saw a leak in the front bedroom as well, and I said to myself, *Oh goodness, that's my room.* What came to mind was if I didn't fix those areas, the second-floor ceilings would sustain damage. I was led to get an estimate although I knew I had no money to pay for roof repairs or possibly replace the roof if I had to do so. Out of obedience to God, I called a local roofer and obtained the estimate. I told him I expected funds to come in but wasn't sure when they would be released. Once I had money in my hands, I would call back to schedule the required work.

Many months later, while I was still in the mist of my job search, the phone rang. When I answered, a gentleman asked for me by name and after I confirmed I was who he was looking for, he proceeded to say his office had been notified that my husband had passed, and he expressed his condolences. He then proceeded to tell me that his company had a policy that my husband had established to cover a possible need for long-term care. He then went on to confirm my address and the spelling of my name because the funds would be sent to me as beneficiary.

I was in total shock because I didn't know that my husband had set anything up. Throughout our marriage, he developed one medical situation after another. He had made sure that provisions were established so he would be taken care of long-term and would not put a financial burden on our family.

I asked the gentleman how much the policy was and when he told me the amount I started to cry. I apologized for the tears, but I briefly explained, the entire situation with the unexpected passing of my husband had made a bad situation worse. I then asked how much I would receive after the taxes were taken out.

He said, "You will receive what I've quoted because your husband had the taxes taken out ahead of time."

At that point all I could say was, "Thank you, Lord", because that amount, after tithes, would cover the entire replacement of the roof (not just a repair) down to the wood.

When God moves on your behalf He moves in a mighty way. All we have to do is learn to trust him on a ridiculous level. People may not understand your position when it comes down to certain situations. When you follow Christ, people are not expected to understand unless they operate on the same level of faith or close to where you walk.

At this time the sheriff's sale was still pending and I had no solution or monetary funds to cover the enormous outstanding debt. Weeks after receiving the word that, "Can't nobody sell, can't nobody buy", I was given the description of a Caucasian man. He would be tall with a receding hairline, wore eyeglasses, and he would help me with my immediate situation.

I did not know anyone who fit that description and prayed that I would not be so engrossed in trying to figure things out that I missed the message God was sending. One day after taking a break from my job search, the voice of the Lord instructed me to file Chapter 13. I was reluctant to do so because I knew it would appear on my credit report for at least 10 years, and my effort to reestablish credit after the bankruptcy would be difficult.

Nevertheless, out of obedience I went ahead and filed the paperwork, which ultimately on the day before the sheriff's sale, locked everyone out. The clock could not have gotten any closer. The prophet was accurate in her description of the Caucasian man and he turned out to be my bankruptcy attorney. Most of us have experienced prophecy and know that it comes in parts, this is why it's imperative to follow God's instructions to the letter and especially when we don't have the full understanding of what's happening.

I finally received the insurance money, made arrangements with the court, and their appointed trustee to resume mortgage payments and work a plan to repay the delinquent amount. We were able to remain in the house.

As time went on, I was hired by a local bank and worked in their Collections Department. Yes, Collections, of all places. As I was working, I was advised of an opportunity with Homeland Security, which was more in line with my former positions. The background check was extensive but at least I was employed while I waited for my clearance to be granted.

About a year later all was completed, and I was offered the position with Homeland Security. My new position paid more than the bank. I was able to maintain the mortgage payments and use my pension for the recurring monthly expenses. Things were on track and, once again, much of the stress I formally endured was over.

Maintaining faith through that entire ordeal was sometimes impossible, but when you have a promise from God all you can do is remember the promise and remember that He is not a man that He should lie (Num 23:19).

> Don't feel sorry for me.
> I'm a walking miracle.

22. No Amputation

It was the 4th Tuesday in July. I went to work as usual but as the morning progressed, I noticed I was walking a little slower because my left leg was becoming heavy. My colleague and I had scheduled a meeting with our government counterparts. Our office was on the third floor of the federal building, but the meetings were held on the sixteenth floor. Normally, for the exercise I would walk up to the sixteenth floor but because of the way my leg felt I chose to take the elevator.

Ironically, that day the meeting was cancelled so we came back down to the third floor. As I sat at my desk my left leg kept swelling from the ankle up. I decided I needed to leave and seek medical advice. Nothing like that had ever happened to me. I walked into the site manager's office and explained my situation.

She said, "You may have a blood clot. I can see that your leg is enlarged."

I looked at her and responded, "I've never had an issue with a clot but needed permission to leave and see a doctor."

Permission was granted and I immediately left the building. I took the elevator down to the ground level and exited the building. By then, my leg was as heavy as a brick. There was no way

ROBIN M. HAILEY

I could walk down the street to the parking lot and retrieve my car. Since it was summer and the lot had little shade, I always parked at the far end under a scrawny tree that kept the sun from beaming directly on the car during the course of the day.

Under the circumstances, there was no physical way for me to get to my car, so I called the site manager and she had the mailroom supervisor come down and he brought the car to me.

When he saw my leg, he offered to drive me home, but I told him since it was my left leg, if I got into the car, I could drive myself. Little did I know, until later that I should have never been behind the wheel of the car, if the clot had dislodged, it would have traveled to my heart or lungs. Aside from that, I drove a Lincoln Town car, which is a heavy vehicle, and traveled a route that had a lot of pedestrian traffic. An accident would have been catastrophic.

I knew my son would be home that day. He had planned to service the church mixer that needed a good cleaning. As I drove home, I called the house phone and then his cell phone. Every time I approached a red light, I tried the phones again. There was no response. My daughter was scheduled to work that day and since my son had the house to himself, he was able to test the unit and blast music without disturbing anyone. That's why he could not hear the phones ringing.

I made it home safely but could not get out the car and there was still no response to the phones. The Holy Spirit said to call 9-1-1. I spoke to the dispatcher, explained my situation, and she advised me to not move. She would send an officer and put a call in for an ambulance. The officer must have been in the immediate area because no sooner than I hung up he arrived in front of the house.

At that time, my son came to the door because the squad car caught his eye and then he noticed my car parked in the driveway when he knew I should have been at work. To be funny he said at first, he thought maybe I had run a red light or something and brought the police home with me but was horrified when he came outside and saw the condition of my leg.

The EMTs asked all kinds of questions relating to blood clots but I told them I had no previous history of anything like that. As we traveled to the hospital, it was my first time in an ambulance and the most uncomfortable ride I had ever taken. In my spirit, I prayed to God to let all be well.

I said, "Lord remember all the times I did what you asked: the times I got up for prayer; the times I opened the doors to the church even when people didn't show up; and the times, out of obedience, I followed your directions even when I knew I would get in trouble with man and people who just didn't understand. Lord, I trust you to bring me through this. I have faith in you for yet one more situation."

We arrived at the hospital and although it wasn't far from the house it seemed to take forever to get there. Not sure what the staff was expecting based upon what they were told about an incoming patient, but what they saw exceeded their comprehension. The initial observation of the doctors was confirming that I did have a clot; but never before had they seen a limb react the way my leg did. By then it was twice the size of my right leg. The leg looked like it belonged on an elephant and not a human.

Knowing a clot caused the situation, their first line of treatment was to start me on Heparin, a blood thinner. I'd never had that medication before and had no idea what would happen after it was administered.

Next, the doctors consulted the physician network, explained my symptoms, and inquired of other doctors if any had treated a patient with this condition. Their immediate concern was that the immense swelling would suffocate the veins and arteries in my leg causing the muscle tissue to die. Another concern about excessive swelling was compartment syndrome, which would make treatment more difficult because it complicated the situation.

The doctors were advised to perform a Doppler ultrasound to determine the exact cause. Come to find out, this was no ordinary blood clot. It ran the entire length of my left leg. The doctors advised my family that I would have to be admitted while

ROBIN M. HAILEY

they tried to figure out the best way to handle the situation. Time was of the extreme essence.

As I lay in the hospital, days turned into weeks, and weeks turned into months. Who would have thought I would end up like this? Most of the treatment was experimental based upon recommendations from physicians in the network. Each day I would pray and talk to God, I let God know that come what may, I still had faith that I would make it through the illness. My family and friends were nervous, but I was actually concerned for my children. I did not want them to have to bury their Mom three years after funeralizing their Dad.

Medical students asked to follow my case so they could use it as part of their studies and include their findings in term papers. To relieve the swelling, the doctors took me to surgery and performed what is called a fasciotomy (surgical incision) on both sides of my calf, then attached a wound V.A.C. (Vacuum Assisted Closure®) to begin the process of extracting the excessive fluid from my leg. Not long thereafter, my condition worsened because I developed compartment syndrome above the knee confirming that the leg was continuously swelling.

Not depending upon a visual observation, the nurses were instructed to measure the circumference of my leg three times a day. I was taken back to surgery and the same process that was performed on my calf was also performed on my thigh and a second wound V.A.C. was attached.

As doctors became more familiar with the condition they were dealing with, they finally had a name for the illness. It's called May-Thurner Syndrome and it only occurs in less than one percent of the general population. To add insult to injury, pumping me full of Heparin didn't come without consequences because it was later discovered, after numerous blood tests, that my platelet count had dropped to a dangerous level.

I have Heparin-Induced Thrombocytopenia or HIT, meaning I'm allergic to Heparin. It causes my blood to lose its clotting factor and highly increase my risk to bleed out. Heparin was immediately stopped, and another intravenous medication was administered.

HIT is an additional strange phenomenon that only occurs in less than one percent of the general population. For one individual to be affected by both is rare. What are the chances of this occurring? Faith in action was my portion on that day and I asked myself, *Whose report will you believe?"*

Sometimes I wondered where I would have been if I didn't have a relationship with God. I have thought about the sacrifices I have made for the work of the ministry and recognize that it is no comparison to the sacrifice Christ made when He gave His life for me. I had faith to believe that I would not die but live to see the salvation of the Lord, just like Moses told the children of Israel in Exodus (14:13). This entire situation looked so grim and the longer I stayed in the hospital, it just appeared to give the adversary more opportunities to take cheap shots against my health.

Doing all they knew to do; the doctors were not feeling as optimistic as I was about how things would end. My leg was in such bad shape that they were talking about amputation. Medically, they saw no possible way to prevent the existing veins and arteries from being severely damaged by the swelling. The debridement process (when they removed dead muscle tissue) could leave the leg dysfunctional.

As the weeks passed, I encouraged my son and daughter who still lived at home with me, to continue to go to church. Come what may; don't break your relationship with God. When you do, it could take twice as long to restore the relationship and that's if you get back. After one Sunday morning service, they came straight to the hospital to deliver a message spoken through the mouth of the prophet. God said, "No amputation."

My pastor was disturbed about the news she was receiving. It just appeared too often. I was being taken to surgery for one procedure after another but there would be no amputation.

One morning my nurses aid came in to help me freshen up and I asked who was on the other side of the nurses' station making all that noise. One replied, "We're not allowed to discuss another patient's condition but what I will tell you is, her condition wasn't as severe as yours, but they had to amputate her leg."

ROBIN M. HAILEY

All I could do was cast my eyes upward from whence cometh my help (Psa 121:1) and say, "Lord I thank you for your Word and your promise."

No doubt, with the discussions of amputation in the atmosphere, God suffered it to be so that it was never performed on me.

I came to realize that while I was hospitalized, I was an encouragement to the staff and the women with whom I shared a room. Every morning it was my routine to read the Bible, usually out loud, not in a disturbing way but with decency. I like to keep the Word of God circulating in the atmosphere. I always asked each new roommate if they would mind. No one objected but using wisdom, when I realized they were Jewish, I only read from one of the first five books of the Bible, as they refer to as the Torah or the Pentateuch. In whatever situation you are in, rely on the Spirit of God to be your guide; you never know how it will help to inspire other people.

One woman, upon her discharge, thanked me for re-introducing her to the Word of God. She said she used to go to the synagogue on a regular basis but so much occurred in her life that she lost hope in Him. She planned to resume her worship because seeing my attitude contrary to my condition, and in comparison to what she was going through, let her know she had much more to be thankful for than she realized.

She was the same person who demanded the nurses check on me when she saw me shaking uncontrollably. A blood test revealed an infection that had been caused by the pic line in my arm. There are some things people do for you that you don't easily forget. God can use whomever He chooses. In the end, it's all for His glory.

It was more than three months and eight surgeries later that I was ready to be released and transferred to an in-house physical therapy facility. I vividly remember that day because it rained. The EMTs tried to keep me under the awning as we departed the building and headed for the ambulance, but I leaned to one side so that I could feel the rain upon my face.

They said, "No, we're trying to keep you dry."

I replied, "Please understand, I've been confined in the hospital for months and it's refreshing to have the rain hit my face."

Thereafter, they understood but just wanted to make sure I didn't turn the stretcher over or fall off of it.

I stayed at the therapy facility for about two weeks, went home for a month, and then back to the hospital so they could close the fasciotomies (incisions) the doctors had performed on my leg. The leg was almost back to normal size making the procedure possible.

Even with that process, the adversary was working overtime. My second stay at the hospital was only supposed to be five to seven days but turned into three weeks because I developed a staph infection and they had to put me in quarantine. The upper fasciotomies were closable using sutures but due to the numerous debridement processes to remove dying muscle, the only way to close the calf fasciotomies was via skin grafts, which landed me in the burn unit. Burn and skin graft patients receive similar treatment.

At some point in your life when things like this keep happening, you may question yourself, *Where do I stand with God? Did I overestimate my faithfulness and fall short somewhere?* I look at Job. He was a righteous man (Job 1:1). He loved God and God respected him. His test was like none other; he lost all that he had, yet through it all he never charged God foolishly (Job 1:22).

When you know you've done all you can to be pleasing unto the Lord, look at the test as a character-building experience. Going through the test may not be easy, nor pleasant by any means, but the mistake some people make is they get stuck in the test. When you don't lean to your own finite understanding but trust in the Lord with all your heart, things will work out in your favor (Rom 8:28).

One thing I've learned in this life, we don't always go through situations for us, what we experience is for the glory of God. I have good days and challenging days with this leg, and it ultimately suffered deformity after all the procedures. I cannot move my left foot up and down. When I walk, the foot rolls to the left; it's called excessive supination. Without a corrective shoe, it looks like I'm walking on my ankle.

In December 2016, I fractured the fifth metatarsal in the foot because of the supination. Through all of this, I'm grateful because I still have both my legs, I can care for myself, drive, and run small errands. Remaining independent was important to me.

Sometimes, people see me walk and have pity in their eyes. I tell them, "Don't feel sorry for me. I'm a walking miracle. The struggle at times is real but I can make it."

God blessed me monetarily and still supplies all my need according to His riches in glory by Christ Jesus (Phi 4:19). So, all I need to do is continue to be thankful, faithful, diligent in my assignment, and obedient.

23. When Will it be My Turn?

In the year 2000, God blessed me to purchase a car that was about as close to new as I've ever owned. It was a 1998 Lincoln Town car, beautiful dark emerald green color, and fully loaded. The owner of the dealership had been the driver. He was selling it because he wanted a newer model. The car was immaculate inside and out. I was one happy sister the day I drove it off the lot and headed for home. It took weeks for me to get accustomed to such luxury. I've always taken a modest approach in my purchases and would never have dreamed I would own such a vehicle.

One day, shortly after buying the car, I gave two of my co-workers a ride to their vehicles. I was closer to the door and on the lower level. They didn't know I had purchased a new car, always saw me in the old one, and when they got in, they expressed all kinds of wonderful comments about the car.

Then, my boss at that time said, "I didn't think we paid you enough money for a car like this."

Now, of course you know this remark could have been taken one of two ways, but my response was, "I'm a tither and God is good."

Thereafter, nothing else was said about my wages nor the car for the duration of my employment at the research and development company.

Eventually, that company downsized and, as a result, I was unemployed for months, but God still blessed me to cover my car payments. All I could say on a regular basis was, "God, you've been good to me."

Ultimately, a real estate brokerage firm hired me. One afternoon I was driving one of my direct reports to the main campus so she could get a new ID badge. She had been temping and recently hired as a full-time employee. Our building was down the street from a local soft drink distributor, so we were very much aware of all the truck traffic. I was sitting at the light waiting for the arrow to turn green so that I could make a right turn.

There was an 18-wheeler in front of me, but he was closer to the left lane giving the impression that he was going straight. The light turned green for both of us and I proceeded to make my right turn, the truck driver makes a right-hand turn from the left side of the road, the tail end of the trailer caught the driver side of my car. My car was dragged around the corner and pushed up on the curb. All I could say was, "Jesus."

Thank God no one was hurt, the driver insisted he had his signal on, but I said, "No, you didn't. Truck traffic on this road has made us very cautious, and if your signal was on, I would have never moved."

We later discovered that the driver was from Kentucky and not familiar with our area, and most likely after he got to the corner realized he needed to make the right in order to get back on the highway.

It pays to live a life for Christ and maintain faith in God because you never know when an unexpected situation will occur, and your reaction can either make or break you. My coworker called her husband and assured him she wasn't hurt and if she had been in the car with anyone else, she didn't think the outcome would have been the same. She said under the circumstances she was so calm that she didn't say one curse word. That name, Jesus, is the sweetest name I know and will help maintain the atmosphere.

Well here we are fifteen years later, and I've approached God several times about the Town car. I thanked Him for His goodness and blessings. I told Him I've seen where some people are driving their fourth or fifth car, and I'm still driving the same Town car. I'm not ungrateful, but at this time in my life would like a newer car. *When will it be my turn?*

One day while on the computer, the Lord said, "If you want a new car, start looking."

I learned from other instances that when you approach God you need to be specific. One thing I knew was that I wanted another Lincoln and a certified pre-owned one because it would come with a full warranty. Brand new cars depreciate once you drive them off the lot and I did not want to lose money that way. I didn't want to lease a car and then have monthly payments. My mindset was to pay cash. My financial status didn't support paying cash for a car, but I depended upon my faith to make it happen.

After looking at different models, I was attracted to the MKZ with a Bordeaux Red Metallic finish. It was a sharp looking car. My next step was to find a local dealer, test drive the car, and discuss price. Now mind you, I had no money, no job, and bad credit, but a lot of faith. The first dealership had the exact car in stock, but the sales representative felt I was wasting his time since I didn't have any money to put down on the car to neither finance nor buy it outright. He seriously blew me off and I felt bad when I left, but the Holy Spirit encouraged me to go back and do more looking.

A few weeks later, I saw the same type of vehicle at another dealership and signed up for a test drive. Now mind you I still didn't have any money but said, "God, I'm going to trust you with this because you've never misled me."

If you declare that you are a faith walker, by Jove you have to practice what you preach. I had a few extra dollars coming to me and figured I could work out something that would qualify me to purchase the car. My plan was to go on a Friday because it would

ROBIN M. HAILEY

put me closer to first of the month, but the Holy Spirit instructed me to go on Thursday. I was already out of my comfort zone but needed to continue pursuing the car because I asked for it and when I asked, I believed God would make it happen. Once again, faith without works is dead (Jam 2:18, 20, 26).

On the Thursday before Halloween, I went to the dealership and met a very nice young man. In my possession I had all the information acquired from their website regarding the car. He checked their system and saw it was still available. He said that this car had just come in. I guessed it was a two-year lease and normally they don't last long, especially this particular model. I told him I was interested in the car but would not have real money to work with until around the first of the month.

He said, "No problem, would you like to test drive the car?"

I replied, "Yes."

In the meantime, my heart was about to pound out of my chest. He had the car pulled around to the front of the building and we got in. I looked at the dashboard having no clue how to even start it. I said, "Oh, this is interesting."

After he instructed me on starting the car, we pulled out to the highway, went up to the first exit, and turned around. He said their policy not to test drive further than that was implemented because others got out on the highway, panicked, and had an accident. I have to say it was love at first drive. I knew I just had to have this car.

Then things got interesting -- the story of my life more times than many. We went to his office and he asked about leaving a deposit. I told him that I didn't have much cash on me and asked what we could do. He wanted to check my credit report but, under my circumstances, I knew that would fall through, so I declined. He tried to insist but I further declined, knowing the details of my financial state. I didn't want to be embarrassed. In certain situations, you're not mandated to expose that which you desire to retain.

He asked if I had a credit card and I told him, "No, I don't use them. I only have a debit card." It was end of the month and my working funds had been depleted but nothing was overdrawn.

He then asked how much cash I had.

I told him, "About $100." I searched through my pocketbook and came up with $99.

He took the money and went into the other office where someone started the paperwork based upon my deposit. While I waited, he returned and said the finance person would give him a call so that he could pick up the receipt. In his hand he had $19. He said they would hold the car with an $80 deposit; they didn't want me to go back home with no cash.

As we talked, I told him about my faith in God and how God has worked wonders for me in the past. I've driven my Town Car for fifteen years; God has been good to me and so has the car, but my desire was to now have a newer one. I did not plan to trade in the Town Car but give it to my son. It was well maintained and ran well.

He then shared something personal about himself; he was a non-Jewish Christian who grew up in Jerusalem. His family came to America when he was fourteen years of age. As a child he walked on some of the very same streets that Jesus walked. He had faith to know that God allows good things to happen to people He cares about. He went back to the other office and obtained the receipt for the $80 .

It was at that point I asked him if he was scheduled to work on Friday, which would have been the next day. My question resulted from my desire to come on Friday but obeyed God and went on Thursday. He said, "No, but if you need me to come in I can."

As I sat there it took all I could do to hold back the tears. The salesperson had left a second time and came back. He asked if I was okay and I assured him all was well.

He left a third time and returned again, this time with an idea. He said in the interim someone else called to inquire about the car, if another buyer comes in with a larger deposit the dealership is obligated to take it and return my $80 to me. He suggested we fill out all the paperwork to lock the car in my name and remove the vehicle from the available list. I agreed and he left again.

All of it was so unbelievable that I looked up and said, "God, you had this young man reserved for me. I'm glad I didn't do things my way and wait until Friday." As I sat in the office, I was led to look to my right and saw another salesperson. The Holy Spirit let me know if I had waited, that's whom I would have dealt with and his demeanor was unfriendly.

The balance of the paperwork was completed, and I then went to the next office to arrange for paperwork that involved the registration and license plates. I told that gentlemen that I was transferring my plates from the Town Car to the MKZ. As a matter of fact, I ordered a duplicate set of plates because I didn't want to put old plates on my new car and received the new set three months ago. My faith in God pushed me to order the plates in anticipation of purchasing my new vehicle. I know all this sounds crazy, but it was a process to get here and then a continued process to stay here.

As he finalized insurance information and the remaining particulars, once all documents were signed, he proceeded to hand over the key. I said, "Wait, please hold the key, I can't take that car home on an $80 deposit. In my spirit I had to smile, God had just, "wowed" me but using wisdom I asked the dealer to hold the key.

Now remember, all this transpired on a Thursday. I got up Saturday morning, Halloween, and the Holy Spirit said, "Check your account."

I replied, "No money is going in until Monday."

I heard it again, "Check your account."

So, I logged onto the computer and gasped. Money, I didn't think I would see for weeks, was sitting in my account. I quickly got myself together, ran to the bank, and asked for a cashier's check. At first, they didn't want to give me a check for such a large amount because the deposit was still pending, but since my pension was directly deposited from the same source and I've been a good customer for many years, they went ahead and cut the check.

As I sat at the red light, I called the sales rep and told him, "I have the money and I'm coming to get the car."

I hurried back home to catch my son before he left for work and asked him to drop me off at the dealership and he gave me a, "what" look.

I said, "I'm picking up my new car."

He was floored, "What car?"

See, for months I had been saying, "I'm getting a new car." I showed him the new plates when they arrived in the mail. You would think after all he's experienced down through the years this occurrence should have fallen in place with everything else, but he didn't believe. This is why there are times you have to keep the vision to yourself; be like Habakkuk (2:2), "Write the vision, make it plain." Then the vision will be revealed at the appointed time (2:3).

He dropped me off at the dealership and went to work. I picked up the car and when I drove it off the car lot, I owed no man anything. God is good all the time. I experienced yet another manifestation of His glory. If I had insisted on leaning to my own understanding (Pro 3:5) by going on Friday instead of Thursday, I would have missed a blessing. I would not have connected with God's chosen sales representative; the funds would have been tied up and someone else would have drove off with the car God had purposed for me. 1 Samuel (15:22b), "Behold, to obey is better than sacrifice."

24. Monumental Faith in Action

Time marched on and the impending issue of being unemployed and not knowing when or if I would be able to go back to work was hanging over my head. The mortgage on my recent house was behind once again and the house went into default. The only option I had through this entire ordeal was to trust God.

One day I had a conversation with Him and said, "Lord, I know, you knew all this would occur when I signed my name on the dotted line to purchase this house." Based upon that, Lord I will continue to hold onto your promise that, "Can't nobody sell, can't nobody buy." God's word states, He is not a man that He should lie (Num 23:19). So, if He said it, He will honor it (Isa 55:11).

Last time I was in this position I filed bankruptcy, this time I had no contingency plan, but my personal endeavor was to remain faithful to God to the best of my ability. I've learned down through the years that God honors a sacrifice and I've developed a cliché that, "God is faithful to the faithful."

Some people think it's all about the money, but God is pleased when He sees that you've made an asserted effort to sacrifice your time and put Him first. I encourage people to spend quality time with God, shut in with Him, commune with Him, block out people, phone calls, and interferences that will interrupt that time.

Now we fast-forward six years, the house has been in foreclosure for this entire period and now the bank is driven to get this house off their books. For an extended period, their attorney would send foreclosure documents stating if the arrears cannot be satisfied and mortgage payments resume as scheduled, the house would be put up for sale.

Sheriff's Sale is Official

Just before Christmas, I received notification that a sale date of January 24th was established with the sheriff's office. I had no funds on hand and nothing expected to immediately come in that would help me settle what was owed, so all I could do was continue to wait on God for His plan. Regarding the 24th, I asked God, what I should do on that day. The Lord said, "Just show up."

Under the circumstances these were strange instructions, but I've personally learned that God's ways are not like our ways, His ways are past finding out (Isa 55:9b). Some people would have replied, "That's seems really crazy, why would I go to sit and watch them sell my house?"

Sometimes God wants to see if we can push past how we feel, what we see and trust Him enough to obey what we don't understand. 1 Corinthians (1:27) let us know that God uses the foolish things to confound the wise. Sometimes you have to just do it, and for heaven's sake, don't tell anybody beforehand, unless you know they support you and will keep you lifted in prayer.

It was a rainy day when I went to the courthouse. For some reason they changed the room and sent people to the far end of the facility. I made my way to the alternate room, which for me was a long painful walk, compounded by a rainy, chilly day. I found the appropriate room, signed in like everyone else and took a seat. Once the proceedings began, the room became very quiet. The sheriff got to my listing and read the property number, stated the address and the upset amount. The upset is the amount the bank was looking to recoup, which at that time exceeded $662,000. When the sheriff read the information, someone asked him to read the upset amount again because they didn't believe what they heard.

At that point there were no bids from those attending the sale and the house was sold to the bank for one hundred dollars. I didn't feel worried about what was next; I just felt optimistic that God would finish the work He began regarding my situation.

As I walked back to my car I sang, "It's raining all around me, I can feel it, it's the latter rain, ride on Jesus, and send the rain, until we are wet, until we are soaked in the latter rain."

As I got to the parking lot a woman walking in the opposite direction said, "Sing, baby." Her comment brought a smile to my face. Sometimes God sends a confirmation to you in some of the most unlikely ways to let you know it's working out for your good.

I figured after the sale, the bank would proceed with what they had to do, up to and including evicting me. Realistically although I had no ability to pay anything on the mortgage, the property was being nicely maintained and they knew it because their inspector sent them a monthly report. Months went by and I began receiving various documents from the bank confirming they now own the property. I was very much aware of that, as the world says, I had no dog in that fight; the battle was God's, and not mine.

I was in a position that required me, for the first time in my life, to operate on a monumental level of faith. At one point I had to ask God, "Why do you deal with me in the area of such big numbers especially when it comes down to money?" Other people would have lost their minds, fell into a deep state of depression, or just gave up and walked away.

God replied, "Because you trust me, and I can trust you." Doubters don't believe you can have a conversation with God, but after you've developed a relationship with Him this is possible. Like I've previously stated, you cannot have a relationship with someone whom you don't spend time with.

ROBIN M. HAILEY

You can't build a solid relationship with your Boo if you don't spend time with that person, get to know them, and allow them to get to know you. Let them get to know the REAL you, sometimes you even have to trust that person with your hurt and surprisingly they can help you through it.

There were days I would walk out in the yard and just look up into the sky and talk to God. As time went on and the weather became milder, I was encouraged to go outside and pray my final prayer for the night. It's not unusual for me to be outside at midnight in prayer because it's quiet; the sky is tranquil and leaves me with the satisfaction that my prayers reach heaven unobstructed.

Sometimes, I had such a need to be under the open heaven when I talked with God I could not stay inside. Praying in the house in a quiet place was okay and going into the prayer room was satisfying, but the real deal was under the open sky where the moon and stars were my covering.

Faith to Move Forward with Upgrades

After the sheriff's sale, the spring season approached, and the township was once again on my case to paint the exterior of my home. It had been in dire need of a paint job for the past few years, but I explained I was working to get it done and needed more time. This was their third warning of which I knew if I didn't do something this time, they would be forced to fine me. There is a city ordinance where homeowners are required to maintain their property because it's an upscale community.

The only thing I could tell the code enforcer was that I was waiting on the approval to move forward, but there was no way I could tell this man that I was waiting on the approval from God. You and I both know that would not have gone over well and I never wanted to give anyone the impression that I was mocking them.

I went back to God asking for further instructions; I said, "Lord, if I get fined, that's money I could have used toward the paint job."

After waiting, God instructed me to obtain estimates for the paint job and replacement windows. My concern was that when the work was completed, it would really bring attention to the house. If the bank were looking to sell it as it appeared before the paint job, they really would take an aggressive approach to sell because it looks better and they could ask for more money.

The year before, I had a similar concern about repercussions from the bank when I purchased my car; my greatest apprehension was, would the bank feel I'm playing a game with them? Will they expedite the process and have the sheriff show up with a locksmith? My concerns were legitimate, but I could not allow them to supersede God's promise.

The first week in May, the painters began sanding off the old paint and I placed an order for the new shutters, the old ones were aluminum and I didn't think they would paint well, plus I had a forth window in front of the house on the second floor that I included in the count for the new shutters.

During that same time, the preliminary measurements were taken for the replacement windows and sliding doors so that I could obtain an estimate. The surveyor provided me with a fresh survey so that I could have the replacement fence installed. Hurricane Irene damaged the original wooden fence and then Hurricane Sandy destroyed it.

People said I should have reported it to my insurance company and they would have helped to pay for the new fence, but that claim would have sat on my policy and I found it was to my advantage to just pay the money and replace it out of pocket.

Request to Vacate

The week of the 4th of July put me on high alert. On the 3rd I received the 90-day notice to vacate, which had been sent by the bank. On the 5th, the constable showed up and I spoke with him.

I told him, "Life is real and it's not over yet. I'm working a contingency plan but not in a position to go into details."

As I spoke with him, I could see him wiping his eyes, he understood what I was saying and was touched by the way I was handling the situation. He was kind enough to share a little of his story as to how things were before he became a constable. He lost his job and business slowed down for his wife and she had to close shop. In the end they lost everything and had to start all over again, so he understood what I was up against and wished me all the best.

I replied, "Thank you. I know you mean well. You're just doing your job."

The next day the local bank representative showed up at my door, he was arrogant. He asked if I had started looking for a place to go and had I started packing? I told him no, I'm working a contingency plan. He wanted to know what my plan was; I told him it wasn't up for discussion at this time. I sent documents to the bank and the property manager asking they give me at least the 90 days.

Little did I know my situation would well exceed the 90-day deadline by more than an additional 9 months. I was a little shaken after my conversation with him, but the Holy Spirit reminded me that God said, "You take care of the small bills and I'll take care of the mortgage." Those were the words He spoke to me on New Year's Day, right after I ended my personal 6:00 AM prayer.

I apologized to the bank rep for speaking to him from the 2nd floor window, but I was still in my nightshirt and not dressed to come to the door. As I spoke with him, I maintained my tone of faith, people who don't understand this walk would perceive it to be denial but the approach of each is entirely different. I told him even with the best laid plan's things happen and sometimes we have no control over what has occurred. Miracles still take place and I believe I will be one of them.

Later that day my son told me someone was there taking pictures of the house; I was dressed and able to go out and greet him. He too was surprised at my cordiality. In these cases, the last thing they want to do is interface with the homeowner/occupant because people can be hostile and threatening. He said he's been watching the house for months and saw the transformation. Under the circumstances he could not figure out why someone would paint a home and replace windows when the property as a result of the sheriff's sale was in the hands of the bank. I told him I believe the report of the Lord and that's what I'm standing on.

My House is Being Auctioned

A week later, I was on the computer and the Holy Spirit led me to look up my address. When I did, I saw where the property had been put up for auction. My heart dropped. In the interim the words of the Lord spoken by the prophet reminded me, God said, "Can't nobody sell. Can't nobody buy." I could have never fathomed that things would get to this state, but still believed it was all in God's plan.

Through the entire ordeal, part of my prayer was, "God don't let me be embarrassed in front of my neighbors, the church family, or my biological family."

Now at this point, the only people outside of my son and two daughters who knew I was in this situation, were my pastor and a very dear friend in Georgia. During our 6:00AM, prayer on the prayer line occasionally my pastor would say, "No one who trusts in the Lord will ever be ashamed" (Psa 25:3).

Since we were on mute, I would reply, "Thank you, Lord for hearing my request and acknowledging my concern."

Thereafter, I thanked God for the leading of His spirit because now it allowed me to monitor what was going on with the property. Each posting lasted seven days and if no one submitted a bid, or if the bank did not accept the bid, the house would be listed again.

Every time they re-listed it, I would bind the listing and any subsequent bidders. I was working hard in the spirit. It had been more than 9 months since the first listing and the house was re-listed 26 times with different starting bids.

At one point, there were more than 1,100 views but the house could not be sold. The bank decided to change the property number and upgrade the online picture hoping to attract more interested parties. With that change, the view count started with the number one and worked its way up each time the site was accessed.

I had seen the starting bid go up and then come down, not sure how they decided where to start the bid, but nothing was working. Each time they re-listed the house I spoke into the atmosphere, Lord, you said, "Can't nobody sell. Can't nobody buy." Every time I unlocked the door to go out and unlocked the door to come in, I would repeat the word God spoke to me.

Recently, at the end of one of our Life Class sessions, Apostle Huffman looked at me and said God said, "He wants you to pray three times per day like Daniel did: morning, noon, and evening. You're almost there."

I reverence the servants of God who allow God to use them to speak into our lives. There are a lot of prophets in the land, you could say a dime a dozen but only a few are true prophets who don't prostitute the gift God has given them and use it for personal gain.

You're Being Evicted

Not long after that session, I experienced another heart dropping situation. My email is set up to send me notification from USPS letting me know what's coming to the house. I saw an image of an envelope with the Sheriff's office as the return address. I said, "Oh no, this can only mean one thing."

I was correct; it was an official eviction notice. Never in my life have I ever been evicted, and this entire process was uncharted territory for me.

The scheduled date was February 7th, basically 15 business days from the day I received the notice. I looked up and said, "Okay God, now what?"

But, there was no immediate response. I later realized that because the news was a shock leaving me in a mental dilemma, God knew if He had given me instructions, I would have missed a step or two.

First Sunday was the 4th of the month. As I prepared for Sunday school, the Holy Spirit encouraged me to go back and look at the notice sent from the Sheriff's office. I read where if I wanted to request an adjournment, I had to file my document with the Chauncey office. As an additive, I was also instructed after the Sunday service, to take a trial run to the building. I found this to be an excellent idea because it gave me an opportunity to go directly to the building and also seek a place to park my car.

Downtown is very busy and if you are not use to that type of aggressive driving it can become frustrating because you get in the way of other motorists who are familiar with the area or in a hurry.

Service was very good as our pastor had ministered from Deuteronomy (10:12), where Moses conveyed the requirements God had for His people, "And now, Israel, what doth the LORD thy God require of thee, but to fear the LORD thy God, to walk in all his ways, and to love him, and to serve the LORD thy God with all thy heart and with all thy soul." God doesn't ask much of us and he doesn't set us up to fail.

After service I headed for downtown. It was a smooth trip; I basically know the area, but the trip allowed me to avoid missing the entrance to the parking garage that happened to be a short distance from the Superior Court building. It was outrageously windy the day I went to the court building.

ROBIN M. HAILEY

For some reason, those buildings create a wind tunnel affect dropping the temperature and causing one to have difficulty walking. Thank God I had my cane, as I cautiously took my steps, a huge gust of wind came by and almost knocked me down. I believe if it were not for the cane, I would have fallen.

I went into the building, placed my belongings on the conveyor to get through security and headed for the directory. I knew where I was supposed to go but didn't see it listed so I went to the information desk at the center isle and asked the gentleman who was sitting there. Of course, he was into his cell phone and acted like I was disturbing him. I told him why I was there, but I guess I didn't give the proper term because his reply was, "You need to go to the County Courthouse."

I raised my eyebrows because

(1) I passed that building on my way to Superior Court; and

(2) my document specifically stated I should go to the Superior Court building.

I walked out the building and the Holy Spirit said, "Stop, that didn't sound right. Look at the notice and make a call."

So, I walked back to the area just outside the door, where I could make my call but stay out of the wind. I first called the person whom I had spoken to the week before, for some reason I didn't want to call the department lieutenant whose number was also listed. She was snippy and condescending, but my resolve was to get past that and ask her a question. Her phone rang and there was no answer, so I called the lieutenant's number and could not reach him either.

The Holy Spirit said, "Go back inside and ask someone else". So I did, and the officer I passed the first time did a double take looking very puzzled. I told him I should be there but was not sure where to go.

I stated my purpose and he replied, "Oh, you need the office on the 8th floor."

I walked through the metal detector once again, gathered my belongings, and headed for the elevator. Once I arrived at the Chauncey's office, I explained to the woman behind the counter why I was there. By the sound of her voice, her attitude, and demeanor, I could tell she was the person I spoke to on the phone the prior week.

Her first question was, "When was your house sold?"

When I gave her the date, she gave me a WHAT look as though she didn't hear me correctly. She then asked for the address and looked it up on the Sheriff's site and told me it had been sold to the bank.

I replied, "Yes, that occurred last year on January 24th."

She then asked if I had already submitted two adjournments and I said, "No, I didn't understand this was an option available to me."

She gave me the form and I sat in the hall to fill it out.

As I wrote, I asked God to tell me what I should say under the area that asks why I'm requesting an adjournment. I didn't rush the answer I just sat and waited.

I was pleased with the information given by the Holy Spirit and was led before I took the form back to the Chauncey clerk to photograph both pages with my cell phone. It was an area where people were allowed to use their phones and there was no objection although I felt a little awkward.

I went back to the waiting area and sat for almost 90 minutes, I watched people come and go and I ended up being the last person whose name was called. In the interim, it gave me time to commune with God. I felt in my spirit even if I saw someone I knew, that wasn't the time to chitchat.

The sheriff on duty called my name and I was led in to see the judge. He went through his formality and advised me a representative from the bank's legal firm was on speakerphone. The judge asked why I was filing an adjournment and in short, I explained my situation. He asked where I'd looked, and for other details.

He then gave the attorney an opportunity to speak; you could hear the anger in his voice at the very prospect that I had the audacity to request an adjournment. I told both the judge and the lawyer that I'm still working my contingency plan and have requested an additional 30 days or equivalent of 4 weeks. My ultimate goal is to buy the house from the bank.

Much to the surprise of the attorney, the judge granted me 5 weeks and stated he liked the way I handled myself. I would have until March 14th to work a definitive plan and the Writ of Possession date is the 1st of May. I thanked the judge so much and thanked Jesus as well; this session didn't necessarily have to end in my favor.

Henry and Ben

A month after obtaining the adjournment an unannounced individual (who going forward, I'll refer to as Henry) rang my doorbell although the listing said, "Occupied, do not disturb."

He said he was an investor interested in buying the house and placed a bid that had been accepted by the bank and he had a contract from them. I had been tracking the activity online and asked his initials because I knew the initials of the highest bidder once the listing reflected, "Reserve met."

He told me his initials were H.F., which let me know he was who he said he was. Much to his surprise, I was more on top of what was going on than he figured I would be, under my circumstances.

He wanted to know what my intentions were regarding the property and I told him I wanted to keep the property but at this time didn't have the funds to satisfy the requirements of the bank. I asked him if, once he closed, it would be possible for me to rent from him until my funds became available to buy the house back and he said we could work something out.

He informed me that he works with a team who helps individuals reestablish credit and obtain a new mortgage. We exchanged phone numbers to make it easier to stay in contact and share information.

I then contacted my attorney because I needed her on standby to review a possible agreement between me and the prospective buyer. I didn't want to sign anything that would have adverse effects in this situation. Four days after speaking with Henry, I was led by the Holy Spirit to go back to the Chauncey division of the Superior Court and apply for a second adjournment.

I ended up seeing the same judge, who was surprised that I was once again standing in his courtroom. I gave him a brief explanation of the recent chain of events and that someone had placed a bid which was accepted by the bank and he was willing to let me rent once he closed.

Based upon the change in my circumstances he approved the second adjournment. He said that, in the five years that he had been on the bench in that division, he had never had a situation like mine.

The bank's attorney fiercely protested. He went on to say that his client wanted me out by March 14th. "Do you know how long she has been in that house? And the bank wants this property off their books."

As a result of the kindness and consideration of the judge, I had until the 23rd of April, to work with Henry, and once our agreement was settled, we could uninvolve the sheriff.

After speaking to a few brokers, Henry sent me a text message that he was no longer interested in renting, because after doing a few upgrades to bring the property up to a more current period, he could ask more than $900,000 for the house. Basically, although the residence had been well-maintained, the interior décor was outdated, leaving it stuck in the 70's.

I was taken back by all this because his attitude was the exact opposite of the conversation we had at the front door. I told him that I had obtained a second adjournment from the court that would buy me time with the sheriff while I worked with him.

He felt betrayed, implying that I had gone behind his back and seen the judge without him.

That was a Friday. I let him know that I didn't need him to go with me. Plus, all he had was a contract. Between him and the bank, there was no exchange of money and nothing was binding.

On Monday, Henry went to the court trying to obtain information about the adjournment, but no one would speak to him. I told him the adjournment was between the bank and me and no, the court would not release any details to him.

I went back to my attorney because at this point, he was trying to play games to obtain access to see the interior of the house.

Each time he asked I said, "No", but never told him I had spoken to an attorney who advised me I had the right to refuse him entrance.

We must be wise in business transactions and stay in a place to hear the voice of God. The attorney confirmed what God had told me: because Henry no longer wanted to rent but buy, upgrade and sell, I would not have a leg to stand on if I allowed him access.

Because he had a contract, he thought it would give him certain rights but like I told him, "Anything can happen before you close so, no, you cannot step foot inside."

He then threatened to get the police to come by with him and then I would have to let him in.

I told him that because of the adjournment, the police would not get involved. I then told him, "Even if you close, you cannot gain access while the adjournment is in effect."

He was livid!

The next evening, Henry sent me a text asking if he could stop by sometime that week with two brokers to see the interior of the home. It would help him with his process.

Once again, I said, "No."

At that point he was infuriated. He said, "Even if you now had the money, I would not sell you the house; I have seven people interested in buying the house once I close and upgrade. You said you are not in a financial position to buy, so please let's not waste time on this. Thanks, and good luck."

I cannot tell you how I felt. All the while, I kept telling myself, *God made me a promise, "Can't nobody sell. Can't nobody buy."*

Three days later, I received another text from Henry, "How are you?"

I didn't reply because he insulted me in his last message. I've learned that in some situations a response is not mandated.

The next day, I received yet another message, "How are you?"

My reply was, "Regardless of what may come, I'm still more than a conqueror through Him that loved me" (Rom 8:37).

Although you may not feel like it, there are times it really pays to be tactful. You never know when your words may come back to you and you want them to be appropriate.

Later, I received another text from Henry stating that he was willing to pay me to allow him to see the interior of the house. He said, "All I need is five minutes."

My answer was still, "No," but I could feel the desperation in the context of his message.

He then sent another message, "I'll give you $500 for five minutes."

I said to myself, What in heavens name is he thinking? God, he has no idea what that sounds like. Am I a $500 whore?

Of course, you know I still told him, "No."

Not long thereafter I received a call from an individual I'll call Ben. He stated that he is entering into a contract with Henry and

ROBIN M. HAILEY

wanted to make arrangements with me to see the interior of the house. Henry told him that I was a nice person and would be willing to work with him. I could tell he was trying to bushwhack me, not realizing he was set up. Henry knew I would not budge, and no one would be allowed access to the interior of the house.

I told Ben that on several occasions I'd said, "No," to Henry and the answer remained, "No."

Ben was angry and said, "After I enter into the contract, I'm coming by with the sheriff."

I told him the sheriff would advise him that they would honor the adjournment issued by the judge, and then I hung up.

Later that afternoon I received a text from Henry. He said, "I wish we could have come to an agreement. Give me your last and best offer. I have someone who wants the house and Monday wants to go into a contract, but honestly, I feel like selling to you. It will be a better move since you are already in the house."

I did not answer right away but waited until the next day and replied, "I know, but without immediate funds, I'm not in a position to make a commitment to purchase and fulfill it."

My answers to him were consistent and honest. He was playing an ugly game. I felt he was insulting my intelligence.

Low and behold, a week later, the Holy Spirit said, "Look up the address."

I went onto the Internet and saw that the, "Reserve Met," ribbon had been removed. The status was, "Listing Currently not Available."

That lead me to believe that there was no deal between Ben and Henry, and the bank was required to put the house up for auction once again. I had figured something was amiss because Henry was trying too hard to get inside. I came to realize he didn't have all the money and was trying to get a mortgage or a business partner to help make up the difference.

Once again, the house was under active auction with the starting bid eleven thousand dollars less than the previous amount. When the auction ended, only one person submitted a bid and that was for the starting amount.

The bank had been trying to sell the house for nine months. I believe those who had been tracking the property were tired of looking at it to the point they were no longer bothering to bid. Of course, after a few days, the house was relisted again with few viewers.

As of the time I wrote this passage, I was still waiting for God to give further instructions. Time was going by, and it was now the 19th of April. The sheriff was scheduled to show up on the 23[rd,] and I had yet to pack a box, in my effort to stand on God's promise.

25. The Ultimate Move

I've experienced on various occasions where God has shown up at what appeared to me as the eleventh hour (a cliché that refers to the last possible moment), but this time it was different. Today was the 23rd of April and I was working in my home office. I looked out the window and saw this big truck not quite in front of the driveway, but then it pulled off and went down the street.

I said to myself, *Oh goodness, are these the people who have been sent to move me out?* Up to that point I had not heard anything more from the third heaven, so I figured that was it.

The truck came back and one of the men rang the doorbell asking if this was the address documented on his paperwork and I confirmed that it was. At this point the sheriffs' vehicle drove up with two officers inside. I was full of mixed emotions and anxiety. I looked up into the sky and said, "But God, you made me a promise."

The officers advised me that this was final. I had no more adjournments and needed to surrender the property. The men were there to help pack my belongings.

I told them I understood and basically said I did all I could to stay, but it just didn't work out that way. They could see I wasn't looking to be combative or hostile to anyone. I told them I appreciated them not arriving in that white car with the big star on the side of it.

They kind of laughed and one of them replied that they understand these situations are sensitive and approach it in a way that leaves the families with as much dignity as possible. They had recently shown up at the home of a couple that had lived there for 50 years. They have a job to do but no one knows how they feel afterward. In some cases, this process is heartbreaking, but it must be done so the bank can take total possession of the property.

Although things looked bleak, God was still working in the mist of us. My eviction paperwork originally said they would send a van, not a truck, but there we were with a truck, bubble wrap, boxes, and three extra men to help pack.

Not fully knowing how things would pan out, months prior, I had obtained a storage unit and moved some of my belongings out of the house. My son has a lot of electronic and sound equipment and I told him, he needed to purge and pack. If the time came for us to vacate, we would have to do it quick, fast, and in a hurry.

I was between a rock and a hard place with the decision to get the storage unit because I was still standing on God's Word that, "Can't nobody sell. Can't nobody buy."

I asked God, "Will this decision to obtain the storage unit give the impression that I don't believe and trust you?"

But God was silent.

Based upon the impending outcome I obtained the unit.

On moving day, to house our remaining items I was given a second unit prepaid for the first month. It was hectic and tiring. Just about everything I wanted had been removed from the house but there were still other items that would not fit on the truck. Coming down to the end of the day the truck had to leave and take our stuff to storage, the facility closed at 6:00 PM with no extension, exceptions, or grace period.

We were now looking at another situation. There were electronics and other personal items left and I definitely didn't want to put them on the side of the house with hopes of coming back to retrieve them the next day.

When the truck returned, the moving Foreman said he could see we still were not finished "This is what we'll do, you continue to remove from the house what you want and when you're done lock the door. Be mindful, once you close the door you cannot go back in; that's it."

In my spirit I said, "Thank you Lord because you're still making a way. Regardless of the circumstances, it takes incredible faith to recognize the hand of God working on your behalf. If you can look beyond the circumstance and still see God, that's amazing.

With such a blessing in our hands we had to figure out where to securely put the remaining items. My son and a friend went to U-Haul to get a trailer, but all the trailers were open, and we needed one enclosed so that our possessions could be locked up overnight.

When they came back, I asked, why he didn't get a truck.

My son said, "Well, Mom, I didn't have the money."

I replied, "So, why didn't you call me?"

We then left instructions for the people who were still at the house and ran to U-Haul only to meet the employees coming out the door. The office had closed for the day.

When you're dealing with conditions such as this, the only thing you can do is retain your faith and remain composed. If you lose your cool, there is no way to hear God when He speaks. When at all possible, keep your emotions intact and don't panic.

We asked one of the employees if there were any other locations still open, and he said, "No, we all close at the same time, but there is an option to go online and request a truck for immediate pickup."

With this information in hand, we started making calls. What a cumbersome process, but after about an hour we were able to obtain keys for a truck from the lock box and went back to the house. We were gone for so long those who were left behind figured we were unsuccessful. Because we were using our cell phones to complete the transaction online, there was no time to give anyone an update.

God, through automation, symbolically had a ram in the bush just for us just like he had for Abraham (Gen 22:13). When looking uncertainty in the face, all you can do is depend upon God.

At this point my oldest daughter had showed up to help with the final packing and walkthrough. It was heartbreaking when she first arrived, especially since I had not said a word to her during the course of the day as to what was transpiring at my home.

She owns a cleaning company and knew what to look for in the final clean sweep. I was so exhausted, there was no way I could make another trip to the second floor or down to the basement, so she did it for me. She pulled out items I would have been upset to leave and was able to put them in her vehicle for safekeeping.

The remaining items were loaded onto the U-Haul truck and I locked up the house for the final time.

Now, we had to find a place to sleep for the night.

26. The Place God Reserved

After getting a good night's sleep, early the next morning I began making a lot of phone calls. First, I terminated all services associated with the house. I didn't want others coming in and creating expenses that, at the end of the day, I would be responsible to pay. I then started looking for an apartment. Because my son and daughter still lived at home, a three-bedroom unit was needed.

I spent a lot of time at the library looking up listings and used my cell phone at other times. I really struggled through this process because typically my cell phone usage was limited to making and receiving calls as well as sending and receiving text messages.

I never felt comfortable using it for Internet activities or banking, but my current situation forced me to do so. I only had 1-GB of data and blew through it real fast. I used a lot of discretion with my activities because I did not want to place myself in a position to have my personal information hacked.

I had narrowed down my search to three towns to avoid becoming frantic in this process. I needed something soon because I could not stay in a hotel for an extended period of time and neither could my son impose on his friend extensively. Fortunately, there was a computer in the lobby of the hotel and hardly anyone used it, so I had additional Internet access when the library was closed.

I would sort through listings, acquire addresses of those within the general area, and do a drive by to see if the accommodations would be appropriate. In some cases, the descriptions and pictures on the Internet were detailed enough to provide the information I was looking for.

To my dismay, many of the rental units were on the 2nd floor and parking at most locations would turn into a nightmare. I needed a first-floor unit so that I could bring in groceries or other items by myself if no one else was home. The incident with my left leg created residual issues that I've learned to work through, but living on the second floor would create a physical hardship.

As it so happened, in the town in which I lived, there was a street that I would frequently take to get to the supermarket. It allowed me to bypass the congestion in the center of town.

I had looked at this place many-a-times because there were two huge *For Rent* signs in the window of the 1st floor apartment. Before the actual move, I had contemplated calling the property manager to see if the apartment was still available, but once again questioned if this was the right thing to do especially since I was still waiting on God to move on my behalf.

Now that I needed a place to live, I called the number and spoke to the individual who identified himself as the property manager. My concern with moving forward was the condition of my credit. I knew everything was tore up from the floor up so to speak, and I didn't know what type of results would surface.

The first thing was to see the interior of the apartment and that I did. The place was small but freshly painted, all it needed was a good cleaning because the sheetrock work left it extremely dusty. I told the property manager that I was seriously interested in renting the apartment and he asked when I would be available to move in. I had to choose my words wisely because I didn't want to divulge my current situation and open the door for a lot of unnecessary questions.

I went online and filled in all the appropriate documents answering all the questions honestly and submitted the information. That, of course, included a credit check. At that point, all I could do was hold my breath and continue to trust God. Along the way I remembered all the times I passed this place and wondered why it was still vacant; *Was God holding it for us?*

Now someone would ask, if you had an inkling that you would have to move and be subjected to a credit check, wouldn't you have performed one ahead of time? The thought did cross my mind, but to be honest with you, I was afraid. I know God's word says He has not given us the spirit of fear (2 Tim 1:7), but this emotional roller coaster ride was becoming borderline overwhelming.

Within a few days of submitting my information, the property manager reached out to me and said my credit was very good and everything else had gone through. Hearing those words made me go in and personally check my credit, when I saw the numbers and the score, you could have knocked me over with a feather.

I said, "No way! How in heaven's name did this happen?"

All I could exclaim was, "Lord, I thank you. I know this could not have happened without your hand moving on my behalf."

As days went by, I still shook my head in disbelief. My score was close to excellent. There was nothing negative on my credit report, even after all the previous heartaches and bankruptcy. Isaiah (54:4) reminds us that God will never allow us to be put to shame.

I made arrangements to pay the security deposit and the first month's rent and we were in. Upon access, we did an initial cleaning to get rid of the dust and while things dried, went to Wal-Mart to get something to sleep on. My former residence had a lot of built in amenities that I could not take, so the optimal solution was to restart simplistically and allow the smoke to clear from the move and replenish slowly.

I had no problem sleeping on an air mattress. Although, my daughter cried for two days because she knew I was better than that. I told her that from there we would take baby steps, one day at a time, and assured her that re-establishment would be accomplished.

Paul's words rang in my spirit man; whatever state I'm in I've learned to be content (Phi 4:11). I knew my current situation was temporary like residing in this apartment, but it would give me at least a year or two if needed to get back on my feet.

My true desire was that my son and daughter would get a place of their own and at that point I could go for myself. One good thing with that location was that we were able to park all three vehicles on the property. There was no need to obtain a parking permit from the city to park on the street or park in the public garage, which was at the bottom of the block. Praise the Lord.

27. The Shift and Resolution

The hardest thing in this entire transition was explaining to family that I had moved out of the house. No one except three of my four children was aware of the impending situation. I knew the question would be, why pay all that money to have work done on the house when you possibly would have to move?

I asked God this same question in advance and His response was simplistic, yet logical.

He instructed me to do the math, take what I owed on the house, and divide that into what the few upgrades totaled. The amount I paid out equated to less than 13% of what I owed in back payments. I felt a certain obligation to do something and obtain a better peace of mind because in essence I had borrowed money that in the long run I could not repay.

In the end, after the house was sold, the investor entirely remodeled the interior of the house. I figured that would happen because the décor was outdated. From what I saw on the exterior, they removed the sliding door in the kitchen and replaced it with a single-entry door.

In responding to family and friends, my reply was that I acted out of obedience to God. Can you be obedient even when the instructions don't make sense? Can you still be obedient when there is a possibility, you'll experience ridicule or criticism because you've taken a stance to trust God?

I didn't go into debt in getting the work done. There are times God wants to see if you will trust Him enough to move forward and not draw back because of doubt and fear.

One Sunday during our noonday service, my pastor rolled up on me unexpectedly and said, "Elder, God said make up your mind. Do you want a small house with a back yard or a big apartment loft?"

I had to shake my head and laugh within myself because I had that very conversation with God the day before, giving reasons why I could not decide one way or another what I wanted. Whatever I chose, I wanted to be there for a while. I'm not one to do a whole lot of moving, plus the expense can be astronomical.

Do you recall that I said the current apartment was only temporary? I didn't plan to stay more than a year or two. Plus, I had belongings in storage, and I was looking to make other arrangements for those items as well. Most of it belonged to my son. I didn't accumulate much because I don't like clutter.

My biggest investment is my babies. The summer had been very hot, and I wondered what condition they were in because of the heat. I was really concerned after I brought one home and he smelt like a cardboard box; I couldn't imagine what state the others were in even though I wrapped them in plastic. God's "Make up your mind," statement was forcing me to make a decision about my next move.

God went on to say, "When you decide, then I'll do it. You don't have to pray on it, just ask."

I don't know if you've ever been in a position like this. It's exciting but scary. It's the kind of opportunity you don't want to mess up. You don't want to ask for the wrong thing, nor do you want to drag your feet and miss the move of God.

God further said that what happened with my house wasn't failure; He said that it was a shifting. Even now, while writing, I'm teary-eyed, because initially I surely felt like a failure until God said it wasn't my fault.

And now, He reveals His purpose for letting what occurred, come to pass. God made sure I understood it wasn't failure on His part. The devil didn't get involved and nobody threw a monkey wrench in the plan.

God had promised me something and He fulfilled the promise. This was true because I moved from the unfinished HUD house into a beautiful single-family.

But now, spiritually I'm in another place and God needed to get me out of there. He could not ask me to leave because I would not let the house go. I was holding on to the Word He gave me stating, "Can't nobody sell. Can't nobody buy," and I continued to stand firmly on that Word.

When God speaks a Word, it does not return to Him void (Isa 55:11), so He had to change His strategy to get me out of that house.

In the end, I have a little more money than before. My credit looks a heck of a lot better than it ever did. I no longer have the stress that came along with trying to negotiate and retain the property, and I've been happier.

The Lord said, "That was VICTORY."

Victory is the resolution; you cannot claim victory, and nothing becomes resolute. God gave me victory so He could shift me and take me further into ministry to operate in a whole different realm. So, in the end, moving out of the house wasn't a loss, regardless of how it came about, but it was a gain.

The Word holds true where Isaiah 55:8 says, "For my thoughts are not your thoughts, neither are your ways my ways, saith the LORD."

Jeremiah 29:11 goes on to say, "For I know the thoughts that I think toward you, saith the LORD, thoughts of peace, and not of evil, to give you an expected end".

When it looks like things could be done differently, God does it His way because our destiny remains in His hands. There are other things on a personal level I had asked God to do in conjunction with moving out of the house and the move was basically the only way to accomplish it. Yes, God successfully addressed that as well.

28. Max

We moved into what was supposed to be a three-bedroom apartment but was actually a two-bedroom, including a small room that was formally a porch but had been enclosed. As a matter of fact, when we moved out, I cracked up when I saw that inside the makeshift closet of that room was the windowsill from a previously existing window.

The home was a single-family converted to a multi-family, but you could tell the contractors took a lot of short cuts and in many areas failed to properly measure, so hardly anything was level. The disproportion from one room to another led me to believe there may have also been an issue with the foundation. The doors were cut short on either the top or bottom and strips were applied to make up for the poor measuring. What happened to the concept that most contractors follow, "measure twice, cut once"?

I had to use great care when climbing into the bathtub to shower because in front of the tub there was a step that ran the length thereof. Given the situation with my left foot, it naturally rolls to the left when dry and can be scary when it's wet. I always made sure there was a towel on the floor for me to step on when getting out of the tub.

The kitchen was very big and contained a full-size washer and apartment size dryer. There were not a lot of cabinets, but a former entrance had been enclosed and could be used as a pantry. I got creative and put a table in there along with plastic toters to maximize the space and once organized, it worked just fine.

The landlord boasted about a security system that became an actual nuisance. It was not appropriate for a multi-family dwelling. Every time someone opened or closed the front door the system would beep in my apartment. My upstairs neighbor at times would leave for work at 4:00 AM, and by the time I managed to go back to sleep the children would leave for school. If the truth was told, the security system was for the benefit of Mr. Landlord, whom I will call, "Max".

Another perk he advertised was that he paid for Internet, but that was also for his benefit. He primarily lived out of the country especially when our weather was cold. He could monitor coming and going via his cameras that were connected to the Internet and, although we had cable, it was truly basic in every sense of the word. Every month I had to send him a text message reminding him to pay the cable bill so we would have Internet and the children could do their homework.

As part of the tenant agreement, he included a clause whereas the first-floor tenant would send him his mail internationally and he would reimburse the tenant for doing so. I had to wonder what he did with the mail once he received it because many times, he failed to maintain his obligations to the property.

As time went on and we got settled in, things began to happen. It was early May and my upstairs neighbor needed to run her boiler in the morning. She's from a warm climate and didn't like the chill. I'm aware that steam heat will produce some knocking in the pipes because hot water is meeting up with cold vapor, but at 3:30 AM, it sounded like someone was hitting the pipes with a sledgehammer. She felt so bad but said she could not take a shower if her unit was cold and that I understood. It was not her fault the system was partially dysfunctional.

Then we went into rainy season and my kitchen ceiling started leaking. I told Max that he had all this work done to repair the ceiling but unless he did something with that flat roof it would all be a waste. By early summer he returned to the property and performed what he considered maintenance on the roof, but all it did was make the problem worse.

Max then brought over a contractor friend to take a look at the roof and was told the roof was beyond repairing and needed replacing. The contractor gave him an estimate that would include removing the entire deck over the first-floor kitchen and all the rotten wood down to the base. Well, Max wasn't in agreement with the recommendation, nor the price, and told the contractor, "I want you to repair the roof. I'm not replacing anything."

No agreement could be reached between those two because the contractor knew replacing the roof was the optimal decision, but Max was too cheap to pay for it. Attempting to repair the roof would create a situation where he would always be called to address chronic leaks. In the end, it would cost him time and money that, from a business standpoint, made no sense. He knew Max would not pay him for additional services rendered.

The contractor then solicited the opinion of three other professional roofers to take a look and provide estimates. Max rejected all three estimates because their high recommendation was to replace the flat roof. In another attempt to repair the leaky spots, Max used some kind of foil to cover areas where it appeared water was coming through. In essence, it turned out to be aluminum foil.

I'm not a contractor and I wasn't sure what kind of material he used, and I didn't want to be judgmental until we had a few very windy days and some of it had blown off the roof. Yes, it was cheap foil. He didn't even think to use heavy duty. Of course, you know I'm being sarcastic at this point. *Who uses aluminum foil to repair a leaky roof?*

He then used tar to seal spots that showed weakness in the material. Unfortunately, one leak turned into several and then more leaks developed with two being the most serious. The kitchen ceiling had splits in it and one of them emitted black water as a result of his tar repair. Not only was this issue affecting the first-floor kitchen, but it was also damaging the upstairs kitchen floor tiles.

Before returning back to his country, Max walked me through the workings of the boiler and seeing how rusted out it was, I was concerned about the true functionality of this unit. He showed me how to disconnect two wires and reconnect them another way to make the boiler run if it does not respond to the thermostat. That's a huge safety issue.

You never run a heating system like that. They are designed to achieve a certain temperature and then shut off. Bypassing the thermostat is a recipe for a disaster. Every time I had a crazy encounter with this character, I would have to let God know, "I'm maintaining faith in you that the next move will be much better."

Our weather began to cool down and Max left and returned to his homeland with the expectation that the rent would still be paid the first of every month, despite the condition of the roof and chronic leaks in the kitchen. Knowing how ill-maintained the rental property was, and how the terms of the lease made tenants responsible for the maintenance of the appliances, I was led to request the utility company perform a pre-season inspection of the boiler.

At first, I didn't think it would be necessary because Max had assured me it was in good working order and all I had to do was increase the temperature on the thermostat if the apartment wasn't warm enough; but, he wasn't honest in other areas and I didn't trust him. His statement about bypassing the thermostat sent up a huge flag. I knew at that point, I needed to have someone come in and perform a pre-season inspection.

After the technician came out, he checked the boiler and red-tagged it. He said it was cracked and dangerous. "You cannot run it in this condition."

I was like, "Oh Lord, and we're going into cold weather."

I notified Max who had an unholy conniption fit. He asked what I did to the boiler. "If it's broken, you'll have to pay for the repair."

I asked him, "Why would I be expected to pay for something I never used?"

I went back to my pre-move in questions and saw where I was led by the Holy Spirit to ask about the condition of the boiler. I asked, "If the boiler malfunctions under normal working conditions and needs to be replaced that is the responsibility of the property owner, right?"

But if all it needs is to be repaired under normal usage then, according to the rental agreement, that is the responsibility of the tenant. He confirmed this was true.

In my obedience to the leading of the Holy Spirit I had someone check the unit before it was utilized and, hence, could not be held liable for its current condition.

Through all the madness I had to maintain strong faith in the Lord that the Holy Spirit would guide me in making the right decisions and maintaining my composure. Sometimes the enemy will do things to cause you to step out of character, but I kept telling myself I have too much Jesus for this.

I was in a stressful situation where I was still paying my rent and paying it on time, but now dealing with a boiler that was inoperative, along with numerous leaks in the kitchen ceiling. The unit had become basically uninhabitable.

For some reason, Max did not see it that way, but my saving grace was my documentation in capturing the chain of events that led to my final decision. I had also been in contact with the township code enforcer and my concerns were valid. The apartment had indeed become uninhabitable.

Have you ever been in a situation where your gratitude to God was immeasurable because when He told you to do something you didn't hesitate? That is where I was. When you deal with an intimidator remember, "Greater is he that is in you" (1 John 4:4). The strength you acquire from the Word keeps you unshakable.

We were then into colder temperatures. The boiler was shut down in October leaving us with no option but to run a couple of space heaters to stay warm. The place was excessively drafty and the wiring old. It created a situation where if someone forgot to turn off a heater and ran the microwave, we would either trip a breaker or blow a fuse.

Like I mentioned previously, the house was a one-family dwelling converted to a two-family lodging, built in the very early 1900's. The wiring was old, and as a result of interesting circumstances, we found the split between the first and second floor units wasn't a clean one.

Thanksgiving was brutally cold. I figured cooking would help provide additional heat to the unit because the space heaters were ineffective. Being very cautious to not overload anything, I still tripped the breaker. Going into the basement wasn't safe either and more so for me because the stairs were horrible, but no one else was home at that time to reset the breaker.

The upstairs neighbor was running her boiler that was in just as bad a shape as the first-floor unit. If the truth were to be told it should have been red-tagged as well. It chronically leaked and Thanksgiving weekend was no different. A couple of times it let off so much steam it was absolutely scary. We were not sure if it was safe to stay in the house or if we should run for our lives.

I had a major concern because the boilers and hot water tanks were right under my bed. I prayed many a night before going to sleep that we would all be safe and wake up the next morning.

So, we're still taking about Thanksgiving. I made my way to the breaker box but had to walk through water because the second-floor boiler had flooded the basement once again. I told Max this was happening, and he claimed the water was seeping in from the neighbor's property next door. WHAT!! Dude, are you serious?

Anyway, not knowing which one to reset I shut off the entire box and noticed the second-floor boiler stopped working.

I said to myself, "I'll be darned, the second-floor boiler is connected to the first-floor breaker box"!

I reset the main breaker on the first-floor box and the second-floor boiler began to run. I just shook my head and went back upstairs.

The next day the Holy Spirit asked me a question, "Do you realize what you did yesterday?"

I had to think a little and it came to me that I walked through all that water to reset the breaker box. I could have electrocuted myself. I look at this situation as unconscious faith because I never looked at it from that perspective. All I knew was that if I didn't resent the breaker, we would have had absolutely no heat. And on a holiday, it would have been almost impossible to get someone to come out.

Realistically, if a technician came and saw the current condition in the basement, he would have shut off the second-floor boiler as well and everyone would have been on the street.

Now we're into the month of December and Max has made no attempt to rectify the roof / kitchen ceiling situation, nor the non-functioning boiler issue. He tried to tell me how expensive boilers are, and it would cost him what I pay in rent for a year to replace it.

He suggested I look them up and see for myself. He was good for calling my bluff even after all the times I threw him under the bus with his own words. I came to realize he was nothing more than a money hungry bully. He had no intention of fixing anything because my opposition against him was fierce.

Max protested so much I went back to the utility company and they sent out the working inspector to verify whether the first technician's diagnosis was accurate. I asked him how many BTU's the unit was, so that in my suggestions to replace the unit my numbers would be precise. I did some homework and provided Max with conservative numbers regarding replacing the boiler.

He then asked me where I got my information. I told him, "I looked it up like you suggested."

His reply to this information was, "Well, for your own benefit, you can replace the boiler but remove it when you leave and put mine back in place."

WHO DOES THAT? I'm telling you readers; you can't make this up.

When you see that nothing will be reasonably resolved it's time to move. I realized Max was taking this approach because it would force me to move. I had become too much of a challenge and by giving him back his own words I was indirectly calling him a liar.

My younger son and daughter still lived with me and I needed a three-bedroom dwelling once again plus somewhere to park the cars. I would have also liked to have a small yard, somewhere to sit during the summer months but easy to maintain. I remember searching before I moved into this place and it was a challenge to find a residence that was accommodating and anticipated the same challenge once again.

One day while looking on the Internet I saw a listing. It was for a townhouse with three bedrooms, and one and half bathrooms in the next town. It had a parking space very close to the front door and a spot for my son's truck. The yard was small and easy to maintain, so we'd have a spot to sit when the weather is nice. I contacted the realtor and made an appointment to see the place, and realized God had sent me there. Knowing I needed to move immediately, God showed me excessive favor.

True faith will take you into places you could have never imagined. After I took the tour, I told the realtor I would really like to rent the townhouse. She said she had two other people interested in seeing it, but renting is actually based upon who clears the credit and background check and then has the funds to close the deal first.

I told her I had the funds but would just need a day to obtain certified checks from the bank. With this approach I was talking like

I already had the unit. My only concern was someone possibly asking, "Why, after seven months, are you moving?"

I let her know up front I cannot continue to stay in an apartment with numerous leaks in the kitchen ceiling and a boiler that was red-tagged by the utility company in October. Her jaw dropped. I told her I still continued to pay my rent until November, but it wasn't healthy to live there, and the landlord made it evident that he had no plans to neither fix nor replace anything.

As promised, when she returned to her office, she sent me the application and I filled it out right away and returned it electronically. It was no more than two hours later that she contacted me to say, "Your application was approved."

People, you know that's God.

I had already started packing, especially after my decision to not pay the December rent. I told Max I could not continue to stay. He had my security deposit and could use it. I'd be out of there sometime during the first week of January.

I was prepared for him to give me a hard time because my notice was less than 30 days, but he was aware of the horrible condition of his property. He was just being obstinate.

The new place was vacated. Maintenance service came in and did their thing and all we had to do was move in. I'll tell anyone, God is so faithful to the faithful. I encourage you not to be weary in well doing (Gal 6:9), but doing all you know to do to stand (Eph 6:13). Stand on Christ the solid rock and maintain your faith in Him.

Epilogue

When all is said and done, I want to express what the Apostle Paul said in 2 Timothy 4:7, "I have fought a good fight, I have finished my course, I have kept the faith."

I pray this book has stirred up the faith you have that's been lying dormant. Exercise it, challenge it, and prove God according to His Word. Let your faith outweigh your fear.

My prayer is that this book immensely blesses each and every reader and that the stories shared will be life changing. Real life experiences can speak volumes and that you remember, if God can do these things for me, He is more than capable of doing extraordinary things for you also. Seasons come and seasons go, but this is our time, time for us to excel in our relationship with God and truly be partakers of His glory and abundance.

Continue to be encouraged in the matchless name of our Lord and Savior Jesus Christ.

About the Author

Elder Robin M. Hailey is a first-time author who has been known for her unshakable faith in God. She accepted Christ as her personal Savior at a young age, knowing God had a special work for her, but not understanding exactly what it would be.

She has been a Sunday school and Bible study teacher for many years. Children under her tutelage received a solid foundation. There were times adults would sit in her class because they enjoyed her style of teaching.

Elder Hailey graduated from Fairleigh Dickinson University with a Bachelor of Science degree in Business Management. She remains active in ministry, spending time with the seniors in nursing homes, and as a hospice volunteer. She sits at the besides of the sick, reading them Scriptures. The hospice family affectionately calls her, "Mother Hailey."

It has yet to be seen where the Lord will take this awesome woman of God, but rest assured, wherever He does, it will impact many people globally.

Elder Hailey can be reached via email at robinmhailey@hotmail.com, or you can Inbox her on Facebook.

www.ingramcontent.com/pod-product-compliance
Lightning Source LLC
Chambersburg PA
CBHW072008090426
42740CB00011B/2135